Henry Beverley

The Land Acquisition Acts

Henry Beverley

The Land Acquisition Acts

ISBN/EAN: 9783337397319

Printed in Europe, USA, Canada, Australia, Japan

Cover: Foto ©ninafisch / pixelio.de

More available books at **www.hansebooks.com**

THE

LAND ACQUISITION ACTS

(ACT X OF 1870 AND ACT XVIII OF 1885.)

WITH

INTRODUCTION AND NOTES.

By H. BEVERLEY, M.A.,
OF THE BENGAL CIVIL SERVICE.

SECOND EDITION.

CALCUTTA:
THACKER, SPINK AND CO.

1888.

PREFACE TO THE SECOND EDITION.

THE fact that the first edition of this little book has been exhausted proves, I think, that it has supplied a want. In the present edition no pains have been spared to make the work a complete and accurate exposition of the law on the subject of the compulsory acquisition of land in India. The decisions of the various High Courts up to date have been noted in their proper places; the Land Acquisition (Mines) Act of 1885 has been added, and extracts given from other special or local laws having reference to the subject of compensation for land taken or injuriously affected. On the other hand, the rules of the Bengal Board of Revenue have been omitted, my object being to increase the usefulness of the book as a manual of the law on the subject applicable not to one province only, but to the whole of British India.

H. B.

July 1888.

CONTENTS.

	Page
LIST OF CASES CITED	vii—x
INTRODUCTION	1—8
THE LAND ACQUISITION ACT X OF 1870	9—89
GOVERNMENT RULES	90—95
THE LAND ACQUISITION (MINES) ACT XVIII OF 1885	97—111
APPENDIX	113—135
INDEX	137—165

LIST OF CASES CITED.

	Page.
Alexander *v.* West End and Crystal Palace Railway Company ...	86
Ananda Krishna Bose *v.* Verner	59
Appasami Mudali *v.* Rangappa Nattan	70
Ardesar Hormasji Wadia *v.* Secretary of State for India ...	32
Aroomachella Gramany *v.* Velliappa Gramany	63
Atri Bai *v.* Arnopoorna Bai	73
Bamasoonderee Dossee *v.* Verner	62, 63, 72
Barnsley Canal Company *v.* Twill	104
Beckett *v.* Midland Railway Co.	42
Bell *v.* Hull and Selby Railway Co.	43
Bell *v.* Wilson	102
Bengal Coal Company *v.* Maharajah Mahtap Chand Bahadoor ...	67
Bhageeruth Moodee *v.* Rajah Jabar Jummah Khan	70
Bholanath Mullick *v.* Heysham	38, 60
Bigg *v.* Corporation of London	47
Boyfield *v.* Porter	88
Bunwari Lal Chowdhry *v.* Burnomoyi Dasi	69
Caledonian Railway Company *v.* Ogilvy	43, 44, 54
Caledonian Railway Company *v.* Sprot	105
Carey *v.* Banu Miya	38
Carey *v.* Kalu Miya	38
Chamberlain *v.* West End and Crystal Palace Railway Company	43
Chooramoni Dey *v.* Howrah Mills Co.	71
Chundi Churn Chatterjee *v.* Biddoo Bodon Banerjee	16
City of Glasgow Union Railway Company *v.* Hunter ...	49, 56
Collector of Gya *v.* Denonath Roy	79
Collector of Hooghly *v.* Rajkristo Mookerjee	38
Collector of Poonah *v.* Kashinath Khasgiwala ...	34, 37, 54, 66
Collector of 24-Pergunnahs *v.* Nobin Chunder Ghose	28
Croft *v.* London and North-Western Railway Company ...	53
Cromford Canal Company *v.* Cutts	104

LIST OF CASES CITED.

	Page.
Darvill v. Roper	102
Deen Dyall Lall v. Mussamut Thukroo Koonwar	71
Doe d. Hyde v. Mayor of Manchester	21
Duke of Buccleuch v. Metropolitan Board of Works	49, 51, 54, 56
Dwarka Singh v. E. Solano	66
Eagle v. Charing Cross Railway Company	42, 57
East and West India Docks, &c., Railway Company v. Gattke	36
Elliott v. North-Eastern Railway Company	105
Fergusson v. London, Brighton and S. C. Railway Company	86
Furniss v. Midland Railway Company	86
Glover v. North Staffordshire Railway Company	44
Gobind Lall Seal v. Secretary of State for India	72
Godadhur Dass v. Dhunput Singh	15, 68, 70, 72
Gordon, Stuart & Co. v. Maharajah Mahtap Chand Bahadoor	67, 71
Gour Ram Chunder v. Sonatun Das	66
Governors of St. Thomas's Hospital v. Charing Cross Railway Co.	86
Great Western Railway Company v. Bennett	105
Great Western Railway Company v. Smith	104
Gur Pershad v. Umrao Singh	70
Hammersmith and City Railway Company v. Brand	49, 56
Herring v. Metropolitan Board of Works	55
Heysham v. Bholanath Mullick	38, 60
Hillcoat v. Archbishops of Canterbury and York	39
Horrocks v. Metropolitan Railway Company	34
Hurmatjan Bibi v. Padma Lochan Dass	31, 34, 65, 74
Imdad Ali Khan v. The Collector of Farakhabad	28
In re Stewart's Trusts	75
In re Marylebone Improvement Act; Ex parte Edwards	57
In the matter of Tulsee Das Sen and another	60
In the matter of the petition of Abdool Ali	33, 59, 66
In the matter of the petition of H. B. Fenwick	28
Issur Chunder Banerjee v. Sattyo Dyal Banerjee	68
James Hills v. Magistrate of Nuddea	78
Joykissen Mookerjee v. Reazoonissa Beebee	67
Kally Churn Ghose v. Tarinee Churn Bose and Clive Jute Mill Co.	40
Kamini Dabin v. Protap Chunder Sandyal	88
Kashinath Khasgivala v. The Collector of Poonah	32

LIST OF CASES CITED.

	Page.
Khurshedji Nusserwanjee v. Secretary of State for India	85
King v. Wycombe Railway Company	86
Knock v. Metropolitan Railway Company	42, 53
Lee v. Milner	55
Little v. Dublin and Drogheda Railway Company	43
Littler v. Rhyl Improvement Commissioners	57
Lyon v. Fishmongers Company	50
Maharajah Dheraj Mahtab Chand Bahadoor v. Chittro Coomaree Bibee	71
Maharajah Mahtab Chand Bahadoor v. Bengal Coal Company	67
Marson v. London, Chatham and Dover Railway Company	87
Mayor of Blackburn v. Parkinson	88
Metropolitan Board of Works v. McCarthy	44, 47, 48, 50, 51, 54
Midland Railway Company v. Checkley	105
Minto v. Kalee Churn Dass	75
Mohesh Chunder Dutt v. Gungamoney Dossee	71
Moore v. Great Southern and Western Railway Company	43
Morgan v. Metropolitan Railway Company	85
New River Company v. Johnson	54
Nobodeep Chunder Chowdhry v. Brojendro Lal Roy	66
Nuzeeroodden Ahmed v. Railway Commissioners	15
Peari Mohun Mookerjee v. Audhiraj Aftab Chand	70
Penny v. South-Eastern Railway Company	49, 54, 55
Premchand Burral v. Collector of Calcutta	37
Queen v. Brown	40
Queen v. Metropolitan Board of Works	44, 48
Raj Mohun Bose v. East Indian Railway Company	29
Raja Nilmoni Singh v. Rambandhu Roy	63, 66, 73, 76, 88
Ram Chunder Singh v. Jabar Jumma Khan	71
Ramanjen Naidoo v. Rangia Naidoo	72
Raye Kissory Dassee v. Nilcant Day	68, 78
Read v. Victoria Station and Pimlico Railway Company	34
Reddin v. Metropolitan Board of Works	87
Rhodes v. Airedale Drainage Commissioners	55
Ricket v. Metropolitan Railway Company	43, 44, 45, 47, 54
Ripley v. Great Northern Railway Company	43
R. v. Cambrian Railway Company	28
R. v. Eastern Counties Railway Company	43
R. v. Great Northern Railway Company	15

LIST OF CASES CITED.

	Page.
R. v. London and North-Western Railway Company	34
R. v. Metropolitan Commissioners of Sewers	28
R. v. North Midland Railway Company	43
R. v. S. Luke's	42
R. v. Vaughan	55
Salter v. Metropolitan District Railway Company	87
Secretary of State for India v. Sham Bahadoor	59, 73
Senior v. Metropolitan Railway Company	43, 57
Shepherd v. Hills	88
Smith v. Martin	86
Sparrow v. Oxford, &c., Railway Company	87
Srinath Mookerjee v. Maharajah Mahtap Chand Bahadoor	67
Stebbing v. Metropolitan Board of Works	39, 54, 56
Steele v. Midland Railway Company	86
Syud Keramut Ali Mutwalee v. Rajah Suttochurn Ghosal	78
Tapidas Gobindbhai v. B. B. and C. I. Railway Company	53, 55
Taylor v. The Collector of Purneah	28, 29, 52, 86
Tuohey v. Great Southern and Western Railway Company	43
Viraragava v. Krishnasami	75
Yesoba Dumodhur v. Secretary of State for India	73, 78

INTRODUCTION.

The first law on the subject of the acquisition of lands for public purposes in Bengal was Regulation I of 1824 of the Bengal Code, entitled "a Regulation for enabling the officers of Government to obtain, at a fair valuation, land or other immoveable property required for roads, canals, or other public purposes; and for declaring in what manner the claims of the zemindars and of the officers in the Salt Department are to be adjusted in certain districts where lands are required for the purposes of salt manufacture." After the usual preamble (s. 1), the next six sections (2—7) of that Regulation laid down rules for the appropriation of lands for public purposes. Section 8 declared that those rules were not applicable to the removal of obstructions to the navigation of rivers; and ss. 9—15 laid down special rules in regard to lands required by Government for the salt manufacture.

The procedure laid down in ss. 2—7 was briefly as follows:— When "landed estate or other immoveable property or anything thereunto belonging" was required for a public purpose, then, "if there be any hindrance to the purchase of the said property by private bargain," the officer entrusted with the work, or any other officer specially appointed in that behalf, was to proceed to the spot, mark out the land, erect a flag upon it, stick up a notice, and make proclamation by beat of drum, requiring all persons interested to appear, and state their claims or objections; after which a report was to be submitted to Government with an estimate of the value of the property. If the parties objected to dispose of the land, or demanded an exorbitant consideration, but the Government still thought that, on grounds of clear and urgent public expediency, it should be appropriated, recourse was to be had to arbitration. Two arbitrators were to be appointed by the parties, and two more by the Judge, Magistrate, Collector, or other officer whom the Government might commission for the purpose of superintending the arbitration; and these arbitrators chose an umpire.

The arbitrators were not authorized to go into questions of title and apportionment unless the claimants agreed in writing to abide by their decision; but the parties were left to carry the points at issue before the Courts in the usual manner, the award of the arbitrators being final, however, as to the amount of compensation. In cases of disputed possession, or for other sufficient reason to be certified by the arbitrators, the compensation-money was to be invested and held in security until one of the claimants obtained an order of Court for payment. But no dispute touching the property or its possession, nor any flaw in the title of the party by or from whom it was transferred to Government on the award of arbitrators, was to be allowed to defeat or disturb the title acquired by Government. Where the ostensible proprietor agreed to transfer the land amicably, the Government might cause proclamation to be made requiring all persons interested to prefer their claims on or before a certain date; and unless a claim had been preferred in pursuance of such proclamation, no suit could subsequently be brought against Government for either the land or compensation. "But nothing herein contained shall affect the liability of the party who may receive the value of any land or other property transferred to Government without having a good title to the same." No award was liable to be reversed or altered, except by regular suit on the ground of corruption or gross partiality. If the award was approved by Government, the surrender of the property might, if necessary, be enforced by the Magistrate. The costs of arbitration were to be paid by Government.

By Act I of 1850 these provisions of Regulation-law were extended to the Town of Calcutta; and Act XLII of the same year declared them applicable to the case of land taken up for railways. Powers were at the same time conferred for entering upon the land in order to survey or set out the line of any proposed road, canal or railway ; for taking immediate possession when necessary; and for the temporary occupation of land within 100 yards on either side of the centre line of the road, &c. It was also provided that suits and claims for lands taken otherwise than under the Regulation were to be preferred within five years from the passing of the Act, after which period, if no claim had been preferred, the land was to vest absolutely in the Government, freed and discharged from all other claims.

In the Bombay Presidency, Act XXVIII of 1839 (an Act for the regulation of buildings in the Islands of Bombay and Colaba) laid down certain rules, amongst other things, for acquiring land for public purposes in the Presidency-Town (ss. 15—21). The Court of Petty Sessions was authorised to take up and land it required. If the Surveyor's estimate was accepted by the owner or other person in possession, the amount might be paid to him, and the Court thereupon acquired a title to the property. If the estimate was not accepted, the amount of compensation was to be determined by "a jury of twelve indifferent men resident on the Island," whose valuation was to be final and conclusive. This Act was extended for railway purposes by Act XVII of 1850.

In the Madras Presidency, the first law passed on the subject was Act XX of 1852. By that Act a declaration was to be made by Government that the land was needed for a public purpose, and if there was any hindrance to its immediate acquisition by purchase, the Government might thereupon enter on possession, and the land was thenceforward vested absolutely in Government, the liability of the transferror remaining unaffected, as under Regulation I of 1824. The provisions for determining the value of the land were also similar. The enquiry was to be conducted by the Collector or other officer specially appointed. If he and the parties interested agreed as to the amount of compensation and the parties entitled to it, he could pass an award ; otherwise the matter was to be referred to arbitration, and the arbitrators were authorised not only to determine the amount of compensation, but also to decide upon claims thereto, and to apportion it among the parties interested; and their award in this matter could only be set aside in a regular suit. Act XLII of 1850 was at the same time extended to the Madras Presidency. By Act I of 1854 both Acts were extended to the Presidency-Town of Madras.

All these local Acts were repealed by Act VI of 1857, which laid down one law on this subject for the whole of British India. Under that Act the principal modifications of the previous law were as follows:—A declaration that the land was required to be taken by Government at the public expense for a public purpose was to be made under the signature of a Secretary to Government, and such declaration was to be conclusive evidence that the land was required for a public purpose (s. 2). The Collector or other special officer was thereupon to take order for the acquisition of the land (s. 3). After marking out the land, making proclamation and serving notices (s. 4), he was to hold a summary enquiry on a fixed date; and if he and the persons interested agreed as to the amount of compensation, he was empowered to award the same, and if the parties also agreed as to the apportionment of the amount, such apportionment might be specified in the award (s. 5). If none of the parties attended, or if they were unable to agree with the Collector as to the amount of compensation, the matter was to be referred to arbitration (s. 6). If any question of title arose, the person deemed by the Collector to be in possession was taken to be the person interested for the purpose of determining the amount of compensation (s. 7). When the Collector had made an award or directed a reference to arbitration, he might take immediate possession of the land, which thenceforward was vested absolutely in the Government, free from all other estates, rights, titles and interests (s. 8). When a case was referred to arbitration, if the Collector and the persons interested could not concur in the appointment of a single arbitrator, they each nominated one (s. 10); and the two arbitrators so nominated appointed a third to act with them (s. 12). If no claimant attended, or if the persons interested neglected or refused to appoint an arbitrator, then a single arbitrator was to be appointed by the Collector to arbitrate the matter, provided that such single arbitrator was not to be an officer of Government (s. 11). With the written consent of all the persons interested, the arbitrators were empowered to determine the apportionment of the compensation (ss. 14-15). The arbitrators were to be paid reasonable fees (s. 21), which were to be included as costs. Costs incurred for the purpose only of determining the compensation were to be paid by Government, unless the amount awarded did not exceed that tendered by the Collector, in which case each party bore his own costs. Costs incurred in determining the apportionment were to be borne by the parties (s. 22). Compensation might be given for damage done to adjoining land (s. 24), to be specified separately in the award (s. 25). The compensation was to be paid at the time of taking possession, or if this was not possible, interest at 6 per cent. would run from that date (s. 27). But the Collector might, if necessary, defer payment and invest the amount in Government Securities pending an order of Court (s. 29). An award could only be set aside by regular suit on the ground of corruption or misconduct of the arbitrators, and in case of reversal, the matter was again to be referred to arbitration (s. 31). A part of a house or manufactory was not to be acquired if the owner desired that the whole should be taken (s. 32).

Act VI of 1857 was subsequently amended by Act II of 1861, the provisions of which mainly refer to the temporary occupation and use of land, whether or not adjacent to that which was permanently required.

Act XXII of 1863 provided for taking land for works of public utility to be constructed by private persons or companies, and for regulating the construction and use of works on land so taken. It laid down rules for the preliminary proceedings to be taken and the registration of such works, for the taking of lands and the payment therefor, for the construction, inspection and public use of the works, for a Government lien on the works, and for other matters.

These three Acts (VI of 1857, II of 1861, and XXII of 1863) were replaced by Act X of 1870, and an attempt will now be made to indicate very briefly the principal changes introduced into the law by that Act.

It has been seen that, in cases where the Collector and the parties interested could not agree as to the value of the land, the law prior to Act X of 1870 provided that the matter should be left altogether to the decision of independent arbitrators, the Legislature being so careful to avoid the possibility of Government influence, that even when an award was reversed by a Court of Justice, the Court was not authorised to dispose of the question of compensation, but the matter had to be referred to a fresh set of arbitrators. It was found, however, in practice, that arbitrators not unfrequently made exorbitant awards, at times even far in excess of the amount claimed by the parties interested.*
It was, therefore, thought desirable not only that a change should be made in the constitution of the tribunal which was to award the compensation in such cases, but that certain rules should be laid down to regulate the principles upon which the compensation should be awarded. Act X of 1870, accordingly, provides that when the parties cannot agree with the Collector as to the value of the land, the Collector shall refer the matter for the decision of the Civil Court; and for this purpose the Court is to be assisted by two assessors, one to be nominated by the Collector, and the other by the parties. If the Judge agrees with one or both of the assessors, their award is final ; but it is open to the Judge to differ from both assessors, in which case his decision will prevail subject to the right of appeal. The principles on which compensation is to be awarded are at the same time laid down in ss. 24—26. The land is to be assessed at its market-value, but by s. 42 an additional sum equal to fifteen per cent. will be paid by the Collector in consideration of the compulsory

---

* In asking leave to introduce the Bill, Mr. Strachey instanced one case in which the arbitrators had given Rs. 47,400 for a piece of land which the Collector had valued at Rs. 75 ; and another case in which they had awarded Rs. 1,01,400 for what the owner had asked Rs. 31,000.

character of the acquisition. It is also provided that damages may be awarded for severance, for injury to other property, for loss of earnings, and for expenses of removal when necessary. Other matters are specified which are not to be taken into consideration, and certain limits are laid down which the amount is not to exceed in certain cases.

This may be said to be the main distinctive feature of Act X of 1870, but another very important change is that, under the new law, all disputes of right and title in the land acquired must be referred to the Civil Court and decided by the Court in the acquisition-proceedings. Under Act VI of 1857 the person in possession was taken to be the owner for the purpose of determining the amount of compensation, and in case of dispute as to the title, the parties were left to settle their differences in a regular suit. But, under the present law as interpreted by the Courts, no such suit will, in future, be entertained if the plaintiff was a party to the proceedings under this Act.

Both by Regulation I of 1824 and by Act VI of 1857 questions of apportionment might be decided by the arbitrators with the written consent of all the parties interested. Under Act X of 1870, the function of the assessors is limited to assisting the Judge in determining the amount of compensation. Questions of title and of apportionment are to be decided by the Judge sitting alone, and his decision on such questions is open to appeal.

Another important amendment is contained in s. 54, which provides that Government is not compelled to complete the acquisition, even though a declaration may have been issued, unless either an award has been made or a reference directed to the Court.

In case of urgent necessity, the Collector is authorised by s. 17 to take immediate possession of any waste or arable land fifteen days after publication of the notice under s. 9, without waiting for the result of his summary enquiry. A similar provision was contained in Act XLII of 1850, but was omitted from Act VI of 1857. In the Statement of Objects and Reasons, it was said that the provision was borrowed from and analogous to Art. 19 of the French law of 8th March 1810.

Lastly, as already remarked, Act XXII of 1863 has been repealed, and in its place the few general provisions contained in ss. 46—50 of the present Act have been enacted. By these sections power is given to acquire land under the Act for public undertakings conducted by private enterprise, subject to such rules and terms as may, from time to time, be laid down by the Government of India on the subject.

Act XVIII of 1885 was passed with the object of providing for cases in which mines or minerals are situated under the land which it is sought to acquire. Certain provisions on this subject were contained in Act XXII of 1863 (ss. 51-52), but the new Act follows the rules laid down in the English Railway Clauses Consolidation Act (8 and 9 Vict., c. 20, ss. 77—85).

THE LAND ACQUISITION ACT, 1870.

CONTENTS.

Preamble.

PART I.
PRELIMINARY.

SECTION.
1. Short title.
   Local extent.
   Commencement.
2. Repeal of Acts.
3. Interpretation-clause.

PART II.
ACQUISITION.
Preliminary Investigation.

4. Power to enter and survey.
   Power to mark out line.
   Power to clear land.
   Previous notice of entry.
5. Payment for damage.

Declaration of intended Acquisition.

6. Declaration that land is required for a public purpose.
   Contents of declaration.
   Declaration to be evidence.
7. After declaration, Collector to take order for acquisition.
8. Land to be marked out and measured.
   Plan.
9. Notice to persons interested.
   Contents of notice.
   Notice to occupiers.
10. Power to require statements as to names and interests.
    Persons required to make statements to be deemed legally bound to do so.

Enquiry into Value and Claims.

SECTION.
11. Enquiry into value and amount of compensation.
    Tender.
    Power to summon witnesses.
12. Postponement of enquiry.
13. Matters to be considered and matters to be neglected.

Award by Collector.

14. Award in case of agreement as to compensation.
    Award to be filed and to be evidence.
15. Reference where no claimant attends, or if Collector and persons interested cannot agree.

Taking possession.

16. Power to take possession.
17. Power to take possession in cases of urgency.

PART III.

REFERENCE TO COURT AND PROCEDURE THEREON.

18. Collector's statement on reference to Court.
19. Service of notice.
20. Power to appoint an assessor.
21. Determination of amount.
22. Appointment of new assessor.
    Powers of new assessor.
23. Proceedings to be in open Court.
24. Matters to be considered in determining compensation.
25. Matters to be neglected in determining compensation.
26. Rules as to amount of compensation.
27. Record of assessors' opinions.
    Difference on questions of law.
29. Agreement as to amount of compensation.
30. Difference as to amount of compensation.
31. Assessors' fees.
32. Costs of proceedings taken by order of Court.
33. Party to pay costs.
34. Award to be in writing.
    Award to state amount of costs.
    Recovery of costs.
35. Appeal from Judge's decision as to compensation.
36. Provisions of Code of Civil Procedure made applicable.

PART IV.

APPORTIONMENT OF COMPENSATION.

SECTION.
37. Particulars of apportionment to be specified.
38. Dispute as to apportionment.
39. Determination of proportions.

PART V.

PAYMENT.

40. Payment of compensation to whom made.
    Proviso.
41. Payment on making award by Collector.
42. Percentage on market-value.
    Payment with interest.
    Time of payment in appealable cases.

PART VI.

TEMPORARY OCCUPATION OF LAND.

43. Temporary occupation of waste or arable land.
    Difference as to compensation.
44. Power to enter and take possession.
    Restoration of land taken.
45. Difference as to condition of land.

PART VII.

ACQUISITION OF LAND FOR COMPANIES.

46. Company may be authorized to enter and survey.
    Construction of sections 4 and 5.
47. Consent of Local Government to acquisition.
    Execution of agreement.
48. Previous enquiry.
49. Agreement with Secretary of State in Council.
50. Publication of agreement.

PART VIII.
MISCELLANEOUS.

SECTION.
51. Service of notice.
52. Obstruction to survey, &c.
    Filling trenches.
    Destroying land-marks.
53. Magistrate to enforce surrender.
54. Government not bound to complete acquisition.
    Compensation when acquisition is not completed.
55. Part of house or building not to be taken.
56. Payment of Collector's charges by Municipal Body or Company.
57. Exemption from stamp-duty and fees.
58. Bar of suits to set aside awards under Act.
    Limitation of suits for anything done in pursuance of Act.
59. Power to make rules.
    Publication of rules.

THE
LAND ACQUISITION ACT

BEING

ACT No. X of 1870

As amended by Acts No. IX of 1871, No. XII of 1876, No. XIII of 1879, and No. XVIII of 1884.

PASSED BY THE GOVERNOR-GENERAL OF INDIA IN COUNCIL.

(Received the assent of the Governor-General on the 1st April, 1870.)

An Act for the acquisition of land for public purposes and for Companies.

Preamble.

WHEREAS it is expedient to consolidate and amend the law for the acquisition of land needed for public purposes and for Companies, and for determining the amount of compensation to be made on account of such acquisition; It is hereby enacted as follows :—

PART I.

PRELIMINARY.

Short title.

1. This Act may be called " The Land Acquisition Act, 1870 : "

Local extent.

It extends to the whole of British India;

Commencement. and it shall come into force on the first day of June 1870.

Under the Scheduled Districts Act, 1874, this Act has been declared to be in force in the following Scheduled Districts, namely :—The districts of Hazaribagh, Lohardugga, and Manbhum, and Pergana Dhalbhum and the Kolhan in the district of Singbhum (*Gazette of India*, 21st October 1881, Part I, p. 504), and the North-Western Provinces Tarai (*Gazette of India*, 23rd September 1876, Part I, p. 505). It is also included in the Schedule to the Santal Perganas Laws Regulation III of 1886.

2. On and from such day Act No. VI of 1857 (*for the acquisition of land for public purposes*), Act No. II of 1861 (*to amend Act No. VI of 1857*), and Act No. XXII of 1863 (*to provide for taking land for works of public utility to be constructed by private persons or Companies, and for regulating the construction and use of works on land so taken*) shall be repealed.

Repeal of Acts.

All references made to any of the said Acts in subsequent Acts, orders or contracts shall be read as if made to this Act.

A brief summary of the former law is given in the Introduction.

Interpretation-clause. 3. In this Act—

The expression 'land' includes benefits to arise out of land, and things attached to the earth or permanently fastened to anything attached to the earth :

'Land.'

Under Act VI of 1857 the word 'land' was defined to extend to tenements and hereditaments of any tenure, and all houses, buildings, trees or appurtenances thereupon, as well as land. Under the Land Clauses Act, 1845, it has been ruled that the term "lands" does not include easements of an incorporeal nature, but compensation may be obtained if an easement appurtenant to a house is injuriously affected ; and it is to be observed that in several important subsequent Acts the term "land" includes easements without any restriction. The present definition is almost as wide as it is possible to make it. In a case not reported (Reg. Ap. 327 of 1884) the Calcutta High Court allowed compensation for the value of *sand* lying in the land.

As regards mines and minerals, see the Land Acquisition (Mines) Act XVIII of 1885 (*post*), which is to be read with and taken as part of this Act. In England, railway companies are not entitled to the minerals underlying the land purchased by them,. but they remain the property of the original owner, who cannot work them, however, without giving notice to the Company, and the Company then has the option of purchasing them at a fair price. Minerals thus form an exception to the rule that the compensation is to be assessed once for all.

'Person interested.'

The expression 'person interested' includes all persons claiming an interest in compensation to be made on account of the acquisition of land under this Act:

That is to say, every claimant must be treated as a person interested until his claim has been adjudicated upon. So Regulation I of 1824 spoke of persons having *or claiming to have* an interest. By Act VI of 1857 the term included "all persons interested in the land, either for life, or for years, or in remainder, reversion or succession, and all mortgagees, leaseholders or tenants, not being tenants by the month or at will, of such land." A farmer (*ijaradar*) was accordingly held to be a person interested— *Nuzeeroodeen Ahmed* v. *The Railway Commissioners and others*, 1 Hay, 157; Marsh., 91. A zemindar, putnidar or other intermediate tenure-holder, and certain classes of ryots may be persons interested. A ryot with a right of occupancy is a person interested, inasmuch as he presumably holds at beneficial rates, and could not be ejected by his zemindar without compensation. See *Godadhar Dass* v. *Dhunput Sing*, I. L. R., 7 Calc., 585. By the English Statute no person is entitled to compensation who has "no greater interest than as a tenant for a year or from year to year,"—that is, who has less than a year of his term unexpired at the time when he is required to give up possession—*Reg.* v. *Great Northern Railway*, 46 L. J.,

Q. B. 4. By Act VI of 1857, s. 7, when any question arose respecting the title to the land or any rights or interests therein between two or more persons making conflicting claims in respect thereof, the person deemed to be in possession as owner or in receipt of the rents as being entitled thereto, was held to be the person interested for the purpose of determining the amount of compensation, the other person or persons being left to establish their right by suit under ss. 28-30—*Chundi Churn Chatterjee* v. *Biddoo Bodon Banerjee*, 10 W. R. 48. Under the present Act such questions are referred to the Court under ss. 15 and 38.

'Collector.'

The expression 'Collector' means the Collector of a District, and includes a Deputy Commissioner and any officer especially appointed by the Local Government to perform the functions of a Collector under this Act:

'Court.'

The expression 'Court' means, in the Regulation Provinces, the Panjáb, British Burma and Sindh, a principal Civil Court of original jurisdiction,

and in the Non-Regulation Provinces other than the Panjáb, British Burma and Sindh, the Court of a Commissioner of a Division,

unless, when the Local Government has appointed (as it is hereby empowered to do), either specially for any case, or generally within any specified local limits, a judicial officer to perform the functions of a Judge under this Act, and then the expression 'Court' means the Court of such officer:

So much of this section as declares the Commissioner of a Division to be a principal Civil Court of original jurisdiction in Oudh is repealed by Act No. XIII of 1879, s. 2. The words "the Panjáb" were inserted by Act XVIII of 1884, s. 74.

British Burma is to be construed as meaning Lower Burma only. Act XX of 1886, s. 4.

When a reference is made to the Civil Court under Bengal Act VI of 1880, s. 28, in respect of damage caused or likely to be caused by any drainage scheme carried out under the Act, the principal Civil Court of original jurisdiction may, when the amount of compensation assessed by the Commissioners does not exceed one thousand rupees, transfer a reference under Part III of this Act to any Subordinate Judge in the same District, and a reference under Part IV of the Act to any Moonsiff in the same District.

'Company.'

The expression 'Company' means a Company registered under the Indian Companies' Act, 1882, or formed in pursuance of an Act of Parliament, or by Royal Charter or Letters Patent;

'Entitled to act.'

And the following persons shall be deemed persons 'entitled to act' as and to the extent hereinafter provided (that is to say)—

trustees for other persons beneficially interested shall be deemed the persons entitled to act with reference to any such case, and that to the same extent as the persons beneficially interested could have acted if free from disability:

a married woman, in cases to which the English law is applicable, shall be deemed the person so entitled to act, and, whether of full age or not, to the same extent as if she were unmarried and of full age; and

the guardians of minors and the committees of lunatics or idiots shall be deemed respectively the persons so entitled to act, to the same extent as the minors, lunatics or idiots themselves, if free from disability, could have acted.

    A guardian of a minor would probably include a manager of his property appointed under Act XL of 1858; and similarly the committee of a lunatic would include a manager appointed under Act XXXV of 1858.

PART II.

ACQUISITION.

Preliminary Investigation.

4. Whenever it appears to the Local Government that land in any locality is likely to be needed for any public purpose, a notification to that effect shall be published in the local Gazette, and the Collector shall cause public notice of the substance of such notification to be given at convenient places in the said locality.

<small>Power to enter and survey.</small>

Thereupon it shall be lawful for any officer, either generally or specially authorized by such Government in this behalf, and for his servants and workmen,

to enter upon and survey and take levels of any land in such locality:

to dig or bore into the subsoil:

to do all other acts necessary to ascertain whether the land is adapted for such purpose:

to set out the boundaries of the land proposed to be taken and the intended line of the work (if any) proposed to be made thereon:

<small>Power to mark out line.</small>

to mark such levels, boundaries and line by placing marks and cutting trenches;

and, where otherwise the survey cannot be completed and the levels taken and the boundaries and line marked, to cut down and clear away any part of any standing crop, fence or jungle.

<small>Power to clear land.</small>

Provided that no person shall enter into any building or upon any enclosed court or garden attached to a dwelling-house (unless

<small>Previous notice of entry.</small>

with the consent of the occupier thereof) without previously giving such occupier at least seven days' notice in writing of his intention to do so.

5. The officer so authorized shall, at the time of such entry, pay or tender payment for all necessary damage to be done as aforesaid; and in case of dispute as to the sufficiency of the amount so paid or tendered, he shall at once refer the dispute to the decision of the Collector, and such decision shall be final.

Payment for damage.

The distinction should be observed between the notification that land is *likely to be* needed under s. 4 and the declaration that land *is* needed under s. 6.

For penalties on obstruction, see s. 52.

6. Subject to the provisions of Part VII of this Act, whenever it appears to the Local Government that any particular land is needed for a public purpose, or for a Company, a declaration shall be made to that effect under the signature of a Secretary to such Government or of some officer duly authorized to certify its orders:

Declaration that land is required for a public purpose.

Provided that no such declaration shall be made unless the compensation to be awarded for such property is to be paid out of public revenues, or out of some Municipal Fund, or by a Company.

The declaration shall be published in the local official Gazette, and shall state the District or other territorial division in which the land is situate, the purpose for which it is needed, its approximate area, and, where a plan shall have been made of the land, the place where such plan may be inspected.

Contents of declaration.

The said declaration shall be conclusive evidence that the land is needed for a public purpose or for a Company, as the case

Declaration to be evidence.

may be; and, after making such declaration, the Local Government may acquire the land in manner hereinafter appearing.

The Act only relates to the acquisition of land needed (1) for public purposes, or (2) for Companies as defined in s. 3. The expression "a public purpose," if it stood alone, would probably be sufficiently general to cover all cases in which land might fairly be taken under the Act; but it is qualified by the proviso under which no declaration can be made unless the compensation is to be paid out of public revenues or out of some Municipal Fund or by a Company. Difficulties have accordingly arisen at times where land was needed for a really public purpose, such as a school or dispensary, the funds for which came from local or private sources. It is a question therefore whether the proviso does not impose an unnecessary, if not a positively mischievous, restriction.

In England it has been held that when land has been taken under the compulsory powers of an Act of Parliament, the Company may be restrained from using it for other than the specified purpose.

By the Tramways Act XI of 1886, s. 7, cl. (3), the Local Government may, in the order for the acquisition of land for the purposes of a tramway of which the promoter is not a company, direct that land may be acquired for the promoter under the provisions of this Act in the same manner and on the same conditions as it might be acquired for the purposes of the Act if a company was the promoter.

The provisions of the Act have been made applicable, either for the purpose of acquiring land or for the purpose of assessing compensation for damage done to land, under various local statutes, an abstract of which will be found further on. In certain cases under these special Acts land may be acquired under this Act for quasi-private purposes. An instance of this is to be found in the Irrigation Acts, when any person desires the construction of a new village-channel, but is unable or unwilling to construct it under a private arrangement with the owners and occupiers of the land affected. See Act III (B.C.) of 1876, s. 52.

It is not absolutely necessary that Government should acquire the land after making the declaration (s. 54).

7. Whenever any land shall have been so declared to be needed for a public purpose, or for a Company, the Local Government, or some officer authorized by the Local Government in this behalf, shall direct the Collector to take order for the acquisition of the land.

After declaration, Collector to take order for acquisition.

8. The Collector shall thereupon cause the land (unless it has been already marked out under section four) to be marked out. He shall also cause it to be measured, and (if no plan has been made thereof) a plan to be made of the same.

Land to be marked out and measured.

Plan.

The Collector must disburse all costs of measurement.

For penalties on obstruction, see s. 52.

It is to be remarked that the Act does not provide for measurement of the land in the presence of the parties interested or for the settlement of disputes as to its area. Any dispute of the kind should be brought to the notice of the Collector at the time of the enquiry under s. 11. In cases of reference to the Court, the extent of the land needed is to be certified to the Court by the Collector under s. 18, and it is doubtful whether the Court would be at liberty to entertain objections as to the measurement.

The Land Clauses Act contains a provision (s. 124) regarding interests in land which have been omitted to be purchased through mistake or inadvertence. As regards defective measurement, see *Doe. d. Hyde v. Mayor of Manchester*, 12 C. B. 474.

9. The Collector shall then cause public notice to be given at convenient places on or near the land to be taken, stating that the Government intends to take possession of the land, and that claims to compensation for all interests in such land may be made to him.

Notice to persons interested.

Such notice shall state the particulars of the land so needed, and shall require all persons interested in the land to appear personally or by agent before the Collector at a time and place

Contents of notice.

therein mentioned (such time not being earlier than fifteen days after the date of publication of the notice) and to state the nature of their respective interests in the land and the amount and particulars of their claims to compensation for such interests.

The Collector shall also serve notice to the same effect on the occupier (if any) of such land and on all such persons known or believed to be interested therein, or to be entitled to act for persons so interested, as reside, or have agents authorized to receive service on their behalf, within the Revenue District in which the land is situate.

Notice to occupiers.

In case any person so interested resides elsewhere, and has no such agent, the notice shall be sent to him by post.

> This section provides for the publication of a *general* notice on or near the land, and for the service of *special* notices on the occupier and other persons interested. The general notice should be published before issue of the special notices.
>
> The notices should state the area and boundaries of the land as ascertained under s. 8, and unless varied in the course of the enquiry under s. 11, the extent of the land certified to the Court under s. 18 should agree with that mentioned in the notices.
>
> As to the mode of service of notice, see s. 51.
>
> By the next section the intentional omission to file a statement of claim is apparently made a penal offence under s. 176 of the Indian Penal Code.
>
> *Entitled to act.*—See definition in s. 3.

10. The Collector may also require any such person to deliver to him a statement containing, so far as may be practicable, the name of every other person possessing any interest in the land or any part thereof as co-proprietor, sub-proprietor, mortgagee, tenant or otherwise, and of the nature of such interest, and of the rents and profits (if any) received or receivable on account thereof for the year next preceding the date of the statement.

Power to require statements as to names and interests.

Every person required to make or deliver a statement under this section or section nine, shall be deemed to be legally bound to do so within the meaning of sections one hundred and seventy-five and one hundred and seventy-six of the Indian Penal Code.

Persons required to make statements to be deemed legally bound to do so.

This section is new, and is found of great use when the parties interested are not known to the Collector.

In order to be able to take criminal proceedings under the latter clause of this section, a period should be fixed in the notice within which the statement referred to should be delivered.

Section 175 of the Indian Penal Code provides a penalty for the intentional omission to produce or deliver up any document to any public servant, and s. 176 for the intentional omission to give any notice or to furnish information on any subject to any public servant. In either case the offender may be punished with simple imprisonment for one month or fine not exceeding five hundred rupees, or both.

Enquiry into Value and Claims.

11. On the day so fixed, the Collector shall proceed to enquire summarily into the value of the land and to determine the amount of compensation which in his opinion should be allowed therefor, and shall tender such amount to the persons interested who have attended in pursuance of the notice.

Enquiry into value and amount of compensation.

Tender.

For the purpose of such enquiry, the Collector shall have power to summon and enforce the attendance of witnesses and to compel the production of documents by the same means and (as far as may be) in the same manner as is provided in the case of a Civil Court under the Code of Civil Procedure.

Power to summon witnesses.

The Collector "*shall* tender such amount to the persons interested *who have attended*." The tender is obligatory if *any* person interested attends the enquiry; and for this reason the Collector is declared to be entitled to his costs when the amount awarded by the Court does not exceed the sum tendered (s. 33).

But the Collector can only make an award if *all* the persons interested have attended and accept his tender (ss. 14, 15).

The Collector should always certify in his statement of reference under s. 18 whether the persons who attended were willing to accept or refused his tender. This information is necessary to enable the Court to judge whether assessors will be required, and also to decide by whom the costs should be paid (s. 34).

For the provisions regarding the summoning and enforcing the attendance of witnesses and compelling the production of documents, see ss. 130 and 159—178 of the Code of Civil Procedure.

12. The Collector may, if no claimant attends pursuant to the notice, or if for any other cause he thinks fit, from time to time postpone the enquiry to a day to be fixed by him.

Postponement of enquiry.

A claimant is properly one who has made a claim, but as the notice requires the persons interested to appear personally or by agent to prefer their claims on the day fixed, the term 'claimant' is probably used as equivalent to 'person interested.'

13. In determining the amount of compensation the Collector shall take into consideration the matters mentioned in section twenty-four and shall not take into consideration any of the matters mentioned in section twenty-five.

Matters to be considered, and matters to be neglected.

See notes under ss. 24 and 25.

Award by Collector.

14. If the Collector and the persons interested agree as to the amount of compensation to be allowed, the Collector shall make an award under his hand for the same.

Award in case of agreement as to compensation.

Such award shall be filed in the Collector's office and shall be conclusive evidence, as between the Collector and the persons

Award to be filed and to be evidence.

interested, of the value of the land and the amount of compensation allowed for the same.

> The Collector can only make an award if *all* the persons interested agree as to the amount of compensation. So, if all the persons interested agree as to the apportionment, the particulars of such apportionment may be specified in the Collector's award (s. 37); but the Collector has no power to apportion the compensation if the persons interested cannot agree among themselves (s. 38). He should, however, point out to them the delay and expense of a reference to the Court, and endeavour to persuade them to come to an amicable settlement.
>
> For the rules as to apportionment, see note on s. 39.

15. When the Collector proceeds to make the enquiry as aforesaid, whether on the day originally fixed for the enquiry or on the day to which it may have been postponed,

Reference where no claimant attends, or if Collector and persons interested cannot agree.

if no claimant attends,

or if the Collector considers that further enquiry as to the nature of the claim ought to be made by the Court,

or if any person whom the Collector has reason to think interested does not attend,

or if the Collector is unable to agree with the persons interested who have attended in pursuance of the notice as to the amount of compensation to be allowed,

or if, upon the said enquiry, any question respecting the title to the land or any rights thereto or interests therein arise between or among two or more persons making conflicting claims in respect thereof,

the Collector shall refer the matter to the determination of the Court in manner hereinafter appearing.

> By s. 11 the Collector is required to enquire summarily into the value of the land, and to determine the amount of compensation. Having done this, he is bound to tender the amount to those persons interested (if any) who have attended, and if they

all attend and accept the amount tendered, he is bound to award it; while, on the other hand, if they do not all attend or refuse to accept the amount tendered, he is bound to refer the matter to the Court. A person interested includes all persons claiming an interest in the compensation, and it may therefore happen that conflicting claims are preferred. In such cases, the law does not empower the Collector to decide between such conflicting claims, but directs that they be referred for decision to the Court. This section, accordingly, states five cases in which a reference is to be made to the Court. In four of these cases the subject-matter of the reference is the amount of compensation; in the last, the determination of the persons who are entitled to it. A further question, the proper apportionment of the compensation among the persons entitled to it, is provided for by ss. 37—39.

The five cases provided for in this section are these:—

(1.) *If no claimant attends.* In this clause, as in s. 12, the term 'claimant' is, probably, equivalent to 'person interested.' If no such person attend, it is impossible for the Collector to make a tender, but by s. 18 he is bound to certify to the Court the amount of compensation he is willing to give; and by s. 19 the Court is also bound in such a case to issue a general notice to all persons interested in the land.

The provisions of the Act which make it obligatory on the Collector to refer the matter to the Court in cases in which the parties interested do not attend, are found to be productive of great delay and inconvenience. As a rule, the reason of their non-attendance is the smallness of the amount at stake. The parties consider that it is not worth their while to attend. The result is a compulsory reference to the Civil Court, and the liability to pay costs which in some cases exceed the amount of compensation. Under the Bengal Irrigation Act III of 1876 (s. 18), if a claimant or other person whom the Collector has reason to think interested omits to attend, the Collector is authorised to fix the amount of compensation, and a reference to the Civil Court is only necessary if objection is taken to the amount within six weeks.

(2.) The next clause provides for a case in which the Collector entertains doubts as to the *nature of the claim* made or the application of the principles laid down in ss. 24—25; as, for instance, where a claim is made for damages, and the Collector is of opinion that the claim should be investigated and the damages assessed by the Court. If any of the persons interested are present, however, the Collector must, by s. 11, make a tender. If the tender is accepted, an award must follow; if it is refused, the case would fall under cl. (4).

(3.) *If any person whom the Collector has reason to think interested does not attend.* The Collector is bound to make a tender to those who are present, though he cannot make an award.

See note on cl. (1) above.

(4.) *If the Collector is unable to agree with the persons interested who have attended as to the amount of compensation.* In this case also a tender must be made.

(5.) *If upon the enquiry any question of title or right arises.* This clause provides for cases in which conflicting claims are made to the land or any rights or interests therein. Such claims can only be decided by the Civil Court. This case is different from that provided for in s. 38, which seems to contemplate an agreement between the parties as to their relative rights and interests, but a dispute as to the manner in which the compensation should be apportioned among them.

The Act is not clear as to how the Court is to proceed in a case where the title to the land is in conflict. The case does not strictly fall either within Part III (which prescribes the manner in which the amount of compensation is to be determined by the Court) or within Part IV (which has reference to its apportionment among the several claimants entitled to it). It is presumed, however, that the Court would in such a case proceed under s. 39, on the ground that if there is a dispute as to the title, there must also be a dispute as to the apportionment of the compensation.

If all the parties present agree as to the amount of compensation, there would seem to be no objection to the Collector making an award, leaving it to the Court to determine the persons who are entitled to it. Under any circumstances he must make a tender (s. 11), and he should state for the information of the Court whether or not it is accepted.

In the first four cases the subject-matter of the reference,—*viz.*, the amount of compensation,—will be determined by the Judge and assessors; in the last case, questions of title, &c., will be tried by the Judge sitting alone. See note on s. 21.

Of course the same case may fall under more than one of these five clauses. For instance, all the persons interested may not be present, those present may not be willing to accept the amount tendered, and may have preferred conflicting claims *inter se*, and at the same time the Collector may consider further enquiry into the nature of the claims to be necessary.

It has been ruled in England, that if the liability to make compensation is denied altogether, the question must be referred to the regular tribunals—*Reg.* v. *Metropolitan Commissioners of Sewers*, 1 El. & Bl. 702. So in *Imdad Ali Khan* v. *The Collector of Farakhabad*, I. L. R., 7 Alln. 817, it was held that where the Collector claims the land as the property of Government or of a Municipality, and denies the title of other claimants, he has no power to make a reference to the District Judge, and the Judge has no jurisdiction to entertain or determine such reference. "Such a position would be inconsistent with the applicability of the Act, for it denies the right of any person to compensation. It seems a contradiction in terms to speak of the Collector as seeking the acquisition of the land, when he asserts that the land is his own, and that no other person has any interest in it." The fact of the claimant being entitled to the compensation he seeks is a condition precedent to his right to avail himself of the machinery provided by the Act. If he has no title to compensation, the whole proceedings before the arbitrator or a jury are *coram non judice*—*Reg.* v. *Cambrian Railway Co.*, L. R., 4 Q. B. 320.

16. When the Collector has made an award under section fourteen, or a reference to the Court under section fifteen, he may take possession of the land, which shall thereupon vest absolutely in the Government free from all encumbrances.

Power to take possession.

Under Act VI of 1857 it was ruled that, "by the 8th section of that Act, the land became vested in the Government absolutely and free from every right or interest therein of whatever description possessed either by the former proprietors or by other persons."—*The Collector of the 24-Pergunnahs* v. *Nobin Chunder Ghose*, 3 W. R. 27;—such as a right of way previously enjoyed by the public over the land—*In the matter of the Petition of H. B. Fenwick*, 14 W. R., Cr. R. 72; 6 B. L. R., Ap. 47—or other easements—*Taylor* v. *The Collector of Purneah*, I. L. R., 14 Cal., 423.

But the compulsory acquisition of land will not justify a nuisance
—*Rajmohun Bose* v. *East Indian Railway Co.*, 10 B. L. R., 241.

The land vests in Government from the date when the Collector takes possession thereof, and it is the persons who are interested in the land at that date who are entitled to the compensation. (Reg. Ap. 232 of 1883, Calcutta High Court, not reported.)

The minerals lying under the land will also apparently vest in the Government unless a statement to the contrary is made under the provisions of s. 3, Act XVIII of 1885 (*post*).

See note on s. 24.

17. In cases of urgency, whenever the Local Government so directs, the Collector (though no such reference has been directed or award made) may, on the expiration of fifteen days from the publication of the notice mentioned in the first paragraph of section nine, take possession of any waste or arable land needed for public purposes or for a Company.

Power to take possession in cases of urgency.

Such land shall thereupon vest absolutely in the Government free from all encumbrances.

The Collector shall offer to the persons interested compensation for the standing crops and trees (if any) on such land; and in case such offer is not accepted, the value of such crops and trees shall be allowed for in awarding compensation for the land under the provisions herein contained.

This section is new, but a similar provision was contained in Act XLII of 1850, s. 5. That Act, however, provided that the amount and distribution of the compensation should be afterwards ascertained—a matter which is left to be inferred in the present section.

Land taken under the Act is taken discharged of all easements, and the loss of easements must be taken into account in assessing compensation for injurious affection—*Taylor* v. *Collector of Purneah*, I. L. R., 14 Cal. 423.

The last clause is not added to the previous section (16), because it is presumed that in that case the crops and trees will be either included in the claim or removed by the owner.

PART III.

REFERENCE TO COURT AND PROCEDURE THEREON.

18. In making a reference under section fifteen, the Col-

Collector's statement on reference to Court. lector shall state for the information of the Court in writing under his hand

(*a*) the situation and extent of the land needed,

(*b*) the names of the persons whom he has reason to think interested in such land,

(*c*) the amount awarded for damages and paid or tendered under sections five and seventeen, or either of them, the amount of compensation tendered for the land under section eleven, or, if no claimant has attended pursuant to the notice mentioned in section nine, the amount of compensation which the Collector is willing to give to the persons interested, and

(*d*) the grounds on which the amount of compensation was determined.

(*a.*) The description of the land should agree with that in the notices under s. 9, or, if there is any variation, it should be fully explained.

(*b.*) The Collector should also give the names of all persons who *claim* to be interested in the land. The residence of each person should also be given as far as possible, in order that there may be no difficulty or delay in the service of notices by the Court.

(*c.*) The object of reporting to the Court the amount of damages awarded under s. 5 is not clear, as the Collector's decision is final.

(*d.*) The 'amount of compensation' in this clause means, of course, the amount which the Collector has either tendered or is willing to give.

19. The Court shall thereupon cause to be served on

Service of notice. each of the persons so named a notice requiring him (if he has not made a claim under section nine) to state to the Court, on or before a day to be therein mentioned, the sum which he claims as compensation for his interest in the land so needed.

The Court shall also cause a notice to be served on the Collector and each of such persons requiring them to appoint on or before a day to be therein mentioned, two qualified assessors (one to be nominated by the Collector, and the other by the persons interested) for the purpose of aiding the Judge in determining the amount of the compensation.

If no claimant has attended pursuant to the notice mentioned in section nine, the Court shall cause to be affixed on some conspicuous place on or near the land needed a notice to the effect that, if the persons interested in such land do not, on or before a day to be therein mentioned, appear in Court and state the nature of their respective interests in the land and the amount and particulars of their claims to compensation, and nominate a qualified assessor, the Court will proceed to determine such amount.

By the first clause of this section the Court has to serve a notice on each person named in the Collector's statement of reference, requiring him to make a claim by a certain date if he has not already done so. Even if he has made a claim before the Collector, this notice must nevertheless be served upon him. By the second clause a notice must also be served upon each of such persons requiring him to nominate an assessor,—the 'such persons' spoken of in this clause obviously meaning the persons named in the Collector's statement, not such of them only as make a claim for the first time before the Court. These two notices may be contained in the same process, and the same date may be fixed for the filing of the claim and the nomination of an assessor. By the third clause a similar notice must *also* be affixed on or near the land in cases in which no person interested has attended the Collector's enquiry.

If it is intended to apportion the compensation-money in the course of the proceedings, under ss. 38 or 39, notice to this effect should also be given—*Hurmutjan Bibi* v. *Padma Lochan Das*, I. L. R., 12 Cal., 33.

If the claim is not made on or before the date fixed, it cannot be admitted unless the Judge is satisfied that there was sufficient reason for the omission (s. 26).

The petition of claim is exempted from stamp-duty by the Court-Fees Act VII of 1870, s. 19, cl. xxii.

As to service of notice, see s. 51.

A qualified assessor.—By Regulation I of 1824 arbitrators were required to be persons of respectability, residents of the pergana or other local division, and impartial. The object of the Legislature in providing that the amount of compensation shall be determined with the aid of assessors is not that each party shall have his own advocate on the Bench, but that the Judge shall have the assistance of practical men of business with local or special knowledge, who, however, should be as independent and impartial as the Judge himself. As Mr. Strachey said in introducing the Bill, the interests of the parties are protected by the presence of assessors, but they should deliberate and act in consultation with the Judge, and the whole proceedings should go on in open Court, so that when the valuation of property is made, all parties interested may know exactly the grounds of the determination arrived at. In *Kashinath Khasgivala* v. *The Collector of Poonah*, I. L. R., 8 Bom. 553, the award was set aside on the ground that the Collector's nominee had a real bias and was therefore not a qualified assessor. The land was being acquired for the municipality, and the assessor in question was not only a rate-payer and an *ex-officio* member of the municipality, but as such had unsuccessfully negotiated with the claimant for the purchase of the land.

The nomination of an assessor should be *in writing*. Act VI of 1857, s. 10, said:—"In every case the appointment (of an arbitrator) shall be in writing, and neither of the parties to the arbitration shall have power to revoke the same without the consent of the other."

An important decision under that Act was given in *Ardesar Hormasji Wadia* v. *Secretary of State for India*, 9 Bom. H. C. Rep., 177.

20. In case of failure to nominate either of such assessors within the time so specified, the Judge shall himself appoint an assessor in his stead.

Power to appoint an assessor.

Regulation I of 1824 provided that each party should appoint two arbitrators; if more than two arbitrators were appointed by the various persons interested, the Judge or other officer concerned was to select two by lot. If only two were nominated, they were to act, no matter whether or not they were nominated by all the persons interested. If only one, then the Judge nominated only one. If none, then the Judge appointed two persons only to arbitrate the matter.

By Act VI of 1857, s.10, if several persons having a joint-interest in the land would not agree in the appointment of an arbitrator, such disagreement was to be deemed a refusal to appoint under s. 11.

If several persons had distinct and separate interests, and they could not agree in the appointment of an arbitrator, the Collector might either make each separate interest the subject of a distinct arbitration, or he might select one of the persons interested to represent the others, and let him make the nomination on behalf of all.

The present Act makes no provision on the subject. If the persons interested cannot agree among themselves as to the nomination, the Judge should probably select the nominee best qualified, having regard also to the value of the various interests affected.

21. As soon as the assessors have been appointed, the Judge and the assessors shall proceed to determine the amount of the compensation.

Determination of amount.

When the assessors have been appointed, a date should be fixed for the hearing of the case.

The function of the assessors is merely to assist the Judge in determining the amount of compensation (s. 19); they have no voice in the decision of points of law (s. 28), or questions of title (s. 39). There is nothing in the Act which gives the Judge and assessors sitting together power to determine the right to compensation, or the title to the land for which compensation is to be assessed—*In the matter of the Petition of Abdool Ali*, 15 B. L. R. 197. Even as regards the amount of compensation, the decision rests with the Judge (s. 30), though if the assessors are agreed, he will probably not differ from them except under special circumstances.

So in England it is not competent to the jury to determine the right of a claimant to compensation. It is for the Court to decide upon the right or title of the party to be compensated, and for the jury to settle the amount, so that the amount has to be tried first, and the title last.—*Reg.* v. *London and North-Western Railway Co.*, 3 El. & Bl. 465; *Read* v. *Victoria Station and Pimlico Railway Co.*, 32 L. J., Exch. 170; *Horrocks* v. *Metropolitan Railway Co.*, 4 B. & S., 315.

It follows from the above that when there is no dispute as to the amount of compensation, it is not necessary to appoint assessors. If none of the persons interested attend, or if all those who appear before the Court agree to accept the Collector's tender, the Judge may at once make an award on the basis of that tender, and proceed, when necessary, to determine the question of title or apportionment.

There is no objection to the Judge trying such questions at the same time that the amount of compensation is being determined, and the practice is generally convenient to all parties concerned—*The Collector of Poonah* v. *Kasinath Khasgiwalla*, I. L. R., 10 Bom. 585. To make two or more cases out of one and the same reference is only productive of additional expense and delay. But due notice must be given of the intention to try these questions in the same proceeding—*Hurmutjan Bibi* vs. *Padma Lochan Das*, I. L. R., 12 Cal. 33.

Under Act VI of 1857, ss. 14-15, questions of apportionment might also be referred to the arbitrators with the written consent of all the persons interested.

From ss. 14-15, it would appear that the Collector is only empowered to make an award if *all* the persons interested agree with him as to the amount of compensation. The Act, however, is not as explicit on this point as it might be, and cases have occurred in which the Collector has agreed with some of the persons interested and has made an award as regards their interest, making a reference to the Court in the case of those persons only with whom he was unable to agree. If the Collector's action in such cases is legal, his award is, of course, binding upon those who have agreed to it, whatever may be the award of the Court as regards the others. If, on the other hand, the Collector's action is illegal, it is presumed that the award of the Court would be binding upon all the persons interested, provided that they have been served with notice under s. 19.

22. If before such amount is determined, any of the assessors dies or desires to be discharged, or refuses or neglects or becomes incapable to act, the party by whom he was appointed may appoint some other qualified person to act in his place.

Appointment of new assessor.

If the assessor so dying or desiring to be discharged, or refusing or neglecting or becoming incapable, were appointed by the Judge,

or, in the case of an assessor appointed by either party, if for the space of seven days after notice from the Court for that purpose the party who appointed such assessor fails to appoint another,

the Judge shall appoint some other qualified person in his stead.

Every assessor so substituted shall have the same powers as were vested in the former assessor at the time of his so dying or desiring to be discharged, or refusing or neglecting or becoming incapable.

Powers of new assessor.

> When a new assessor is appointed after the hearing of the case has commenced, it is not absolutely necessary to take the evidence again *ab initio* (s. 191, C. C. P.) And under no circumstances should either party be allowed to take advantage of the opportunity to set up a new case.

23. Every proceeding under section twenty-one shall take place in open Court, and all persons entitled to practise in any Civil Court shall be entitled to appear, plead and act, or to appear and act (as the case may be), in such proceeding.

Proceedings to be in open Court.

> '*Entitled to practise.*'—This does not, apparently, authorize the appearance or acts of recognized agents under ss. 35—41, C. C. P. Certain agents are recognized, however, in s. 9.

24. In determining the amount of compensation to be awarded for land acquired under this Act, the Judge and assessors shall take into consideration—

Matters to be considered in determining compensation.

First, the market-value, at the time of awarding compensation, of such land :

Secondly, the damage (if any) sustained by the person interested, at the time of awarding compensation, by reason of severing such land from his other land :

Thirdly, the damage (if any) sustained by the person interested, at the time of awarding compensation, by reason of the acquisition injuriously affecting his other property, whether moveable or immoveable, in any other manner, or his earnings ; and

Fourthly, if, in consequence of the acquisition, he is compelled to change his residence, the reasonable expenses (if any) incidental to such change.

<small>Sections 24—26 lay down the principles upon which compensation is to be awarded, the two first sections being applicable to the enquiry before the Collector (s. 13), as well as to that before the Court. The three sections are to be read over to the assessors before they give their opinion (s. 26). Section 24 enumerates four matters that are to be taken into consideration in awarding compensation ; s. 25 enumerates seven matters that are not to be taken into consideration ; and s. 26 prescribes certain rules limiting the amount of compensation in certain cases.

In considering these matters, the remark of Lord Truro in *East and West India Docks and Birmingham Junction Rail. Co. v. Gattke* (20 L. J., Ch. 217) should be borne in mind : —These Acts are to be liberally expounded in favour of the public, and strictly expounded as against the Government or Company taking the land.

(1.) *The market-value at the time of awarding compensation.*
The market-value is the price which an ordinary private purchaser might be expected to give for the property, were the owner desirous of parting with it. There are ordinarily three circumstances which may serve to indicate this market-value—(1) the price at which the land taken, or any part of it, has sold on pre-</small>

vious occasions ; (2) the present rental of the property, which may be capitalized at so many years' purchase ; and (3) the price at which similar land in the neighbourhood has been sold. Auction-sales, as a rule, are not a fair test of the true market-value, the prices obtained being often far above or below the real value of the property.

In *Premchand Burral and another* v. *The Collector of Calcutta* (I. L. R., 2 Cal. 103), it was held that the fairest and most favourable principle of compensation to the owners was to enquire " what is the market-value of the property, not according to its present disposition, but laid out in the most lucrative and advantageous way in which the owners could dispose of it." In that case GARTH, C. J., (MACPHERSON, J., concurring) said that to capitalize the present rental of the property at so many years' purchase was not always a fair way of arriving at the market-value. " When Government takes property from private persons under statutory powers, it is only right that those persons should obtain such a measure of compensation as is warranted by the price of similar property in the neighbourhood, without any special reference to the uses to which it may be applied at the time when it is taken by the Government, or to the price which its owners may previously have given for it. Of course, if it can be satisfactorily shown that the purposes to which the land is applied are as productive as any other to which it is applicable, or that the price given by the owners is its full market-value, it would be very just to assess the compensation upon that basis." It is submitted, however, that, in calculating the value of the land as laid out to the best advantage, the cost of so laying it out would have to be taken into consideration on the other side.

The principle laid down in the case just cited was approved in *The Collector of Poonah* v. *Kashinath Khasgiwala*, I. L. R., 10 Bom. 585, where it was admitted that the most lucrative and advantageous way in which the owner could dispose of the land was by laying it out for building purposes. " The question then is, what would be its market-value if so laid out; and the most reliable evidence on that question must be the rates per square foot at which similar building sites in the neighbourhood have recently been sold."

In many parts of the country transfers of land are of unfrequent occurrence, and the rental forms the only basis on which the market-value can be ascertained. In such cases, however, the rental on which the calculation is based should be a rack-rent payable by tenants-at-will, and not the rates payable by ryots with permanent or occupancy rights. The number of years' purchase at which it should be capitalized will depend on various circumstances, such as the locality and the demand for land, the prevailing rate of interest, and the price of Government securities. A purchaser of land even in the mofussil would probably expect to get at least five per cent. on his investment, while in the case of house-property, in Calcutta say, he would expect eight or ten per cent. to compensate him for the cost of repairs, rates and taxes, and the chance of the property lying unoccupied. "Every case must depend on its own circumstances, on the evidence given, and the nature of the property. The number of years' purchase, which it would be right to allow with regard to one sort of property, might not be a fair allowance for other kinds of property, and we wish to guard ourselves against being understood as laying down any rule as to the number of years' purchase which ought to be allowed "—*Heysham* v. *Bholanath Mullick*, 11 B. L. R. 236. In assessing the value of house-property situated in the town of Balsar, the Court awarded a capital sum which, at the rate of six per cent. per annum, would yield interest equal to the ascertained annual rental of the premises after deducting the amount necessarily expended for annual repairs—*Carey* v. *Banu Miya*; *Carey* v. *Kalu Miya*, 10 Bom. H. C. 34. See also *Collector of Hooghly* v. *Rajkristo Mookerjee*, 22 W. R. 234.

At the time of awarding compensation.—That is, by the Collector or the Court, as the case may be. It sometimes happens that when a reference is made to the Court, the award is not made till some considerable time after the land has been acquired, and the market-value of the land may have gone up in the interval. It has been questioned whether in such a case the persons interested are entitled to have the benefit of any such increase in value. What is intended apparently is, that the land shall be assessed at the value it has at about the time when it is acquired, not at a value it may have commanded in the past, nor at a prospective estimate of what it may command in the future. It could never have been intended that if, between the date of taking possession and the date of award, Government had dismantled valuable buildings standing on the land, compensation should not be paid for such buildings; or that if, after taking possession and before the date of the award, Government had improved the land, compensation should be awarded for such improvements. On the other hand, the fact of the acquisition may cause a rise in the value of all land in the neighbourhood, and there would seem to be no reason why the owners of the land actually acquired should be deprived of the advantage of any such general rise in value. To give an instance: A large tract of land in a thickly populated district is acquired for the purpose of constructing a dock. The acquisition of this land diminishes the area available for dwelling purposes, and sends up rents throughout the district. It can hardly be contended that a person whose land is taken, and who is thereby driven to find a dwelling elsewhere should not receive as compensation at least as much as he would have to pay for a similar dwelling in the neighbourhood. Section 125 of the Lands Clauses Act, 1845, provides that in estimating the compensation to be paid for lands, the purchase whereof may have been omitted through mistake or inadvertence, it is to be assessed according to what it may have been at the time the lands were entered upon and without regard to any improvements or works made, and as though the works had not been constructed. Accordingly it has been suggested that the compensation should be determined under this Act upon the basis of the market-value which the land had at the time possession was taken under s. 16 or s. 17, and not upon the value it has at the time the compensation is awarded.

In *Hillcoat* v. *Archbishops of Canterbury and York* (L. R., 10 C. B. 327) Lord TRURO, C. J., observed that "the value was to be ascertained in relation to the situation of the property generally, and its applicability to ordinary purposes, discharged of any prescribed appropriation." But see *Stebbing* v. *Metropolitan Board of Works* (L. R., 6 Q. B. 37), where in a similar case of a churchyard being taken which had been closed under an order in Council, it was held that the plaintiff was entitled to compensation only for the loss that he had sustained by being deprived of his interest in the churchyard, and not according to the value that the land would be to the defendants after they had acquired it.

(2.) *Damage by severance.*

By the construction of a railway part of an owner's land was taken and several acres were severed from the rest and all access cut off; the land was at the time the railway was constructed agricultural, but it had a prospective value for building—*Held*, that the compensation jury, valuing it as building land, might estimate the damage by severance as if all access were cut off— *The Queen* v. *Brown*, L. R., 2 Q. B. 630.

In an appeal to the Calcutta High Court (301 of 1886, decided on 12th January 1888), *Kally Churn Ghose* v. *Tarinee Churn Bose and the Clive Jute Mill Co.* (not reported), the facts were that a strip of land across the company's premises was taken by a municipality for the purpose of constructing a road. At either end of this strip of land was a public roadway leading to it, and over the strip itself the public had acquired a right of way for foot passengers and animals, though not for wheeled traffic. The mill itself was separated from the strip by a wall which ran along the north of it; but the company possessed some land south of the strip. It was held that the company was not entitled to any damages for severance over and above adequate compensation for the land actually taken. PETHARAM, C. J., said:—" The allegation here is that when the soil over which the old pathway runs, and which for the purpose of what I have to say must be admitted to have been the property of the claimant, has been acquired by the municipality, and a good road wider than the old road has been constructed upon the site of it, then the land on the southern side of it will be injuriously affected, because it will be severed from the rest of the compound. The first question then is, will it be severed from the rest in any different sense than what it was severed before. As I said before, it has always been severed by a wall which is the property of the claimant, and by the strip of land which was also their property, but which was dedicated to the public as a highway in such sense that the claimants could not use the surface of it in any way inconsistent with the right of the public to use it as a highway at all times except for wheeled vehicles. It is clear in that state of things that they could, if they thought fit, take down the wall and lay the whole compound open, so that they may pass and repass across the pathway in any way they chose consistent with the right of the public to use it as a public road. But when one considers what the rights of the public are, the only right which the owners of the land could have would be a right in common with the rest of the world to use it as a highway, that is to say, to use it to pass along it from one end to the other, and across it from one side to the other, so that the condition of things previous to the acquisition of the land by the municipality was that one side of the compound was divided by a pathway 8 feet wide which had to be maintained as a pathway and which could only be used by them for that purpose; and the condition of things when this piece of land has been acquired by the municipality and when a wider and better road has been constructed, will be that one side of the compound will be divided by a good road instead of a bad one. They will still have a right to take down the wall if they think fit, and will also have a right along with the public to pass along the road from end to end, and cross and recross it at any point they please. It has not been shown that any actual damage has been sustained, and the only damage that has been suggested is the possible one that some day the claimants may want to put up a tramway on this land, which possibly they might have done if it had continued a pathway, but which they cannot do now that it has been acquired by the Government. We do not think that is a sufficient ground for saying there is any evidence of any injurious affection whatever by the new works which it is proposed to construct."

(3.) *Damage by reason of the acquisition injuriously affecting the other property of the person interested, or his earnings.*

In order that a person may be entitled to compensation under this clause, two things seem to be necessary:

1*st*. He must be a person interested, or claiming to have an interest, in the land to be acquired.

2*nd*. His *other* property, moveable or immoveable, or his earnings must be *injuriously affected* by the acquisition.

What constitutes a sufficient interest in the land acquired to entitle a person to compensation may sometimes be a matter of considerable difficulty, particularly when the interest is merely an indirect benefit arising out of the land. A person will probably be considered interested in the land to be acquired, and so entitled to compensation, if within certain limitations *any* of his property or his earnings are injuriously affected by reason of the acquisition, even though he himself may neither own nor occupy any of the land actually acquired. The principle in question is borrowed from the law and practice in England, and though it is not possible to reconcile the various decisions on the subject, it may not be without its use to consider some of the more important of them.

It must be remembered, however, that the wording of the English Statutes is different from that of the present Act. Section 68 of the Land Clauses Consolidation Act, 1845, runs to this effect:— "If any party shall be entitled to any compensation in respect of any lands or of any interest therein which shall have been taken for, *or injuriously affected by,* the execution of the works," he is to follow the course therein directed as to having a jury summoned, &c., to determine the amount of compensation. And s. 6 of the Railway Clauses Consolidation Act, 18 45, after extending the provisions of the Land Clauses Consolidation Act, contains these words:—" And the company shall make to the owners and occupiers of, and all other parties interested in, any lands taken or used for the purposes of the railway, *or injuriously affected by the construction thereof,* full compensation for the value of the lands so taken or used, and *for all damage sustained by such owners, occupiers, and other parties* by reason of the exercise, as regards such lands, of the powers " vested in the company. Under these Statutes, the following are the principal of the later rulings:—

In *Eagle* v. *Charing Cross Railway Company* (L. R., 2 C. P. 638), it was held that an easement is an interest in land for which compensation may be claimed under the Land Clauses Consolidation Act. In that case the plaintiff was awarded compensation for a diminution of light caused by the erection of the defendants' works, whereby the plaintiff's premises were rendered less convenient and suitable for the purposes of his trade.

So it was held that the owner of a house and shop adjoining a railway was entitled to compensation for damage sustained by him in consequence of the dust and dirt from the railway works having penetrated his shop and damaged his goods—*Knock* v. *Metropolitan Railway Co.,* L. R., 4 C. P. 131.

In *Beckett* v. *Midland Railway Company* (L. R., 3 C. P. 82), the defendants had erected an embankment on a portion of the highway opposite to the plaintiff's house, thereby narrowing the road from fifty to thirty-three feet, and thus diminishing the value of the house for letting or selling and obstructing the access of light and air to it : *Held,* that this was such a permanent injury to the estate of the plaintiff in the premises as to entitle him to compensation. See also *Reg.* v. *St. Luke's,* L. R., 7 Q. B. 148.

So it was held that the claimant's house was injurlously affected when the public road immediately in front of it was lowered seven feet—*Moore* v. *Great Southern and Western Railway Co.*, 10 Ir. C. L. R. 46; and similarly when the road was raised ten feet—*Tuohey* v. *Great Southern and Western Railway Co.*, 10 Ir. C. L. R. 98; *Reg.* v. *Eastern Counties Railway Co.*, L. R., 2 Q. B. 347. A farm was held to be injuriously affected by the cutting off of a stream that used to flow through it—*Little* v. *Dublin and Drogheda Railway Co.*, 7 Ir. C. L. R. 82. So a wharf by the construction of a railway between it and the river—*Bell* v. *Hull and Selby Railway Co.*, 6 M. & W. 699. So where a colliery was inundated by the diversion of a brook—*R.* v. *North Midland Railway Co.*, 2 Rail. Ca. 1. In *Chamberlain's* case—a leading authority—a railway company made an obstruction and deviation in the public road so that a part of it which ran in front of some newly-built houses was less used as a thoroughfare than formerly, and the houses were thereby rendered less suitable for shops. It was held that they were injuriously affected, and that the owner was entitled to compensation—*Chamberlain* v. *West End of London and Crystal Palace Railway Co.*, L. J., Q. B. 201; 32 *ibid*, 173.

In *Senior* v. *Metropolitan Railway Company* (32 L. J., Exch. 225), the plaintiff carried on the business of a tailor selling readymade clothes exhibited by him in a window of his shop. The company, in the execution of their works, obstructed certain streets, in consequence of which the street in which the plaintiff's shop was situated was less used and frequented as a thoroughfare, and the plaintiff's business fell off. It was held that the loss of trade was an injury to the value of the land itself, and therefore the subject of compensation under the Land Clauses Consolidation Act. This decision was subsequently overruled, however, by *Ricket* v. *Metropolitan Railway Company*.

In *Ripley* v. *Great Northern Railway Company* (L. R., 10 Ch. 435), a railway company took land on which cotton mills would probably have been built, and the owner had other land on which he had built a reservoir from which water might be supplied to such cotton mills when built: *Held*, that evidence was properly taken as to the profits which might have been derived from supplying water to the mills when built, and that compensation was properly awarded for those profits.

In *The Caledonian Railway Company* v. *Ogilvy* (2 Macq. Sc., App. 229) "a public road was, under the sanction of an Act of Parliament, crossed by a railway on a level, and gates were placed across the road; and it was held by the House of Lords that the owner of a house near the newly-erected gates had no claim for compensation for the inconveniences occasioned to him. The owner of the house had no other right over the road than that which belonged to the public generally, and the erection of the gates across the road where the railway crossed it upon a level was essential to the public safety. It was doubtful whether the owner of the house sustained any injury different in kind, though it might be greater in degree, from that of the rest of the public; and therefore it was questionable whether he could have maintained an action if the obstruction had been created without the authority of Parliament. But in *Glover* v. *The North Staffordshire Railway Company* (16 Q. B. 912), the plaintiff had a private way appurtenant to his farm, which was obstructed by the company's works. His land, therefore, was injuriously affected, and as Mr. Justice Wightman said, "supposing no Act of Parliament had passed, and that had been done which was done, an action would have been maintainable"—*Per* Lord CHELMSFORD in *Ricket* v. *The Metropolitan Railway Company.*

In *The Queen* v. *Metropolitan Board of Works* (L. R., 4 Q. B. 358), " the occupier of premises near the Thames had been accustomed to exercise a public right of drawing water from the river and to use a right of way or access to the river for that purpose, and also to resort to and use a public draw dock for loading and unloading barges. In the execution of works authorized by the Thames Embankment Act, the defendants caused an embankment to be erected by which the access to the river was practically cut off, and the access to the dock by barges was attended with difficulty and danger. It was held that the damage complained of was one for which the occupier of the premises was not entitled to compensation; that the injury was of a personal nature, the right interfered with being one which he possessed in common with the public, though, living near, he exercised it more frequently than others. There can be no doubt that that case was properly decided, as there was nothing to show that the rights obstructed were in any peculiar manner connected with the claimant's premises, nor was there any finding that the premises were by the obstruction diminished in value. It is a case precisely similar to that of *The Caledonian Railway Company* v. *Ogilvy*"—*Per* Lord CHELMSFORD in *Metroplitan Board of Works* v. *McCarthy.*

In *Ricket* v. *Metropolitan Railway Company* (L. R., 2 H. L. 175) Lord CRANWORTH said :—" Both principle and authority seem to me to show that no case comes within the Statute unless when some damage has been occasioned to the land itself in respect of which, but for the Statute, the complaining party might have maintained an action. The injury must be actual injury to the land itself, as by loosening the foundations of buildings on it, obstructing its light, making it inaccessible by lowering or raising the ground immediately in front of it, or by some such physical deterioration. Any other construction of the clause would open the door to claims of so wide and indefinite a character as could not have been in the contemplation of the Legislature." In that case the plaintiff was the occupier of a public-house situated by the side of a public footway. In the exercise of their powers, the railway company had temporarily obstructed streets leading to this footway, so as to make the access to the public-house inconvenient, and the plaintiff claimed compensation in respect of the interruption to his business and injury to his trade consequent on those obstructions. Lord WESTBURY expressed the opinion that "the word 'injuriously' does not mean 'wrongfully' or 'unlawfully,' nor does it imply that compensation is limited to cases where the act done is such as, but for the powers given, would be a tort at common law, the words mean 'damnously affected' only." Although Lord Westbury's view was overruled in that and subsequent cases, his remarks may be quoted at length in this place :—

"In an early stage of the judicial exposition of Statutes of this description, Lord Eldon decided that they must be treated as contracts between the Companies and the Legislature. And this is no doubt the true principle by which they should be construed and applied. Liability to make compensation, therefore, is the contract of the Companies with the Legislature; and the right of the parties interested, that is, the parties sustaining loss, results from that contract and the enactments which give effect to it. If this view be correct, it is a mistake to lay down that the injury intended by the words 'injuriously affected' must be one in respect of which, if there had been no Statute enabling the company to do the act, an action would have lain for the injury at common law. Right to compensation is a title introduced by, and dependent on, the Statutes; and it is only necessary to prove special damage to the occupant of the property occasioned by the construction of the railway or its incidental works, and that the complainant is a party interested within the meaning of that phrase in the Statute. I use the words 'special damage,' or individual particular loss, because I entirely concur with the doctrine that compensation cannot be claimed by an individual for damage which is sustained in common by all the subjects of the realm. Thus, if a public highway be diverted or crossed on a level by a railway, the inconvenience of having to wait whilst trains pass is common to all the public; and the benefit which it is considered results to the public from the railway is the only compensation. Persons dwelling in the neighbourhood may sustain this inconvenience more frequently than the rest of the public; but if the inconvenience is to be regarded as compensated by the public convenience, it cannot be converted into a ground for compensation by reason of certain persons having to sustain the inconvenience more frequently than the rest of their fellow-subjects.

"I agree also with the distinction that has been taken between damage resulting from the railway when complete, or from the act of making it, and damage occasioned by the proper (not negligent) user of the railway when made. No claim can be made for loss resulting from the due user of a railway. Many persons, such as the proprietors of stage-coaches, stage-waggons, and the owners of posting-inns, may be ruined by the user of the railway by the public, but they have no claim to compensation. Compensation is given by the Statute only to individuals who, in respect of the ownership or occupancy of lands or tenements, sustain loss in or through the construction of the railway or the erection of the incidental works . . . . . It seems difficult to deny, that the occupier of a public-house, the value of which depends on its custom, has his interest in that house materially damaged by loss of custom. It may always have been used as a public-house, and as such have been let to the occupier who takes it and pays a high rent for it as a public-house. When he took it, its value was ascertained and the rent fixed by reference to the custom it had; and it seems in the highest degree unreasonable to strip the house of its character, and of the use and purpose for which it has been constructed, fitted and employed; and having done so, to say that the interest of the occupier has sustained no damage, because the building or structure has not been deteriorated. A man gives a rent of £100 per annum for a public-house with good custom, long established in some much-frequented thoroughfare, which house, if not used as a public-house, would not be worth £50 per annum. Suppose, then, that the thoroughfare should be wholly or partially obstructed, and the custom of the house thereby diminished by one-half, is it consistent with common sense to say that the interest of the tenant in the house is not materially prejudiced ? It is a fallacy, almost a mockery, to answer, 'the custom is one thing and the house another: and the injury is to the custom, not to the house.' You cannot sever the custom from the house itself, or from the interest of the occupier, for the custom is the thing appertaining to the house which gives it its special character and constitutes its value to the occupier, and for which he pays in the high rent he has agreed to give. If you diminish the custom of a public-house, you diminish its value either to let or sell, and therefore you deteriorate the public-house and the interest of the tenant therein.

"The true principle and the only rule is, that in the enquiry whether the interest of the occupier of a messuage or building is damaged, that is, injuriously affected, you should estimate the value of the messuage or building to the occupier with reference to the use that he makes of it, and the beneficial purpose for which he has hired it and fitted it up, and for which he has paid and pays to the landlord a larger annual sum than the building *per se* would command; and if you find this use and enjoyment impaired by the works of the railway, you are bound to decide that the interest of the occupier is *pro tanto* damaged, that is, injuriously affected."

The principle laid down in *Ricket* v. *Metropolitan Railway Company* was approved by Lord O'HAGAN in *The Metropolitan Board of Works* v. *McCarthy*, and in the same case Lord CAIRNS said :—" The proper test as to the proper meaning of these words as giving a right to compensation is to consider whether the act done in carrying out the works in question is an act which would have given a right of action if the works had not been authorized by Act of Parliament. *I do not pause to enquire whether or not, if the question was now to be decided for the first time, it is not a test somewhat narrow.* I accept that test as being the test that has been laid down and which has formed the foundation for the decision of so many cases before the present."

So in *Bigg* v. *Corporation of London* (L. R., 15 Eq. 376), it was held that the plaintiff was not entitled to be compensated for the indirect injury to his trade resulting from the diversion of traffic caused by the authorized act of lowering the roadway, but only for direct structural injury occasioned by the unauthorized interference with his cellar.

In *The Metropolitan Board of Works* v. *McCarthy* (L. R., 7 H. L. 243), McCarthy was the lessor or occupier of a house in close proximity to a draw dock which opened into the Thames. He had no right in any way to the use of the dock except as one of the public; but his premises being in close proximity to it, his use of it for the purposes of his business was very constant. The dock was entirely destroyed by the works of the Thames Embankment. The case submitted to the Court stated " that by reason of the destruction of the dock and the destruction thereby of the access to and from the Thames, the plaintiff's premises became and were as premises either to sell or occupy in their then condition, and with reference to the uses to which any owner or occupier might put them in their then state and condition, permanently damaged and diminished in value." It was held that the plaintiff was on these facts entitled to compensation. Lord Penzance said :—" The right to compensation will accrue whenever it can be established that a special value attached to the premises by reason of their proximity to, or relative position with, the highway obstructed, and that this special value has been permanently injured by the obstruction." He said that two rules had been established by previous decisions. One was " that whether damage can be recovered under the words '*injuriously affected*' depends upon whether it might have been the subject of an action if the works which caused it had been done without the authority of Parliament;" the other was " that the damage or injury which is to be the subject of compensation must not be of a personal character, but must be a damage or injury to the land of the claimant, considered independently of any particular trade that the claimant may have carried on upon it. This was decided in *The Queen* v. *Metropolitan Board of Works*."

Lord Chelmsford said :—" The learned Counsel for the respondent proposed the following rule as a guide to the decision of each case: Where by the construction of works authorized by the Legislature there is a physical interference with a right, whether public or private, which an owner of a house is entitled to make use of in connection with the house, and which gives it a marketable value apart from any particular use to which the owner may put it, if the house by reason of the works is diminished in value, there arises a claim to compensation. I think the rule as thus stated may be accepted with this necessary qualification, that when the right which the owner of the house is entitled to exercise is one which he possesses in common with the public, there must be something peculiar to the right in its connection with the house to distinguish it from that which is enjoyed by the rest of the world."

In *The Hammersmith and City Rail. Co.* v. *Brand* (L. R., 4 H. L. Eng. and Ir. Ap. 171), it was held that a person whose land has not been taken for the purpose of a railway cannot recover compensation on account of damage or annoyance arising from the vibration caused by passing trains after the railway is brought into use, even though the property has been depreciated. So in regard to the noise and smoke caused by passing trains—*City of Glasgow Union Railway Co.* v. *Hunter*, L. R., 2 H. L. Sc. 78; *Penny* v. *South-Eastern Railway Co.*, 26 L. J., Q. B. 225. But in the *Duke of Buccleuch* v. *Metropolitan Board of Works* (L. R., 5 H. L. 418) it was held, that although compensation cannot be granted to a person annoyed by the smoke and vibration occasioned by trains passing along a railway constructed under the authority of an Act of Parliament when no part of his land has been taken, yet compensation may be given for deterioration in the value of his property occasioned in a similar manner where a part of his land has been taken.

In the same case it was also held that in this question of compensation may be considered a person's particular and individual use of that in which he has no particular right, such as the shore of a tidal river. The plaintiff was the owner of a house and garden on the bank of the Thames; he had had the use of a causeway which ran from his garden to low-water mark in the river and which was always repaired and kept in order by him; he was deprived of the use of this causeway and of his communication with the river by the embankment of the river and the formation of a road between it and the garden. Mr. Justice HANNEN said:—" Plaintiff as owner of land abutting on a navigable river, was entitled to a right of access to the stream along his whole frontage, and not merely at the spot where his jetty projected. If in the course of time it would have been advantageous to the plaintiff to use the whole of the land abutting on the Thames as a wharf or for any other purpose, he would have been entitled to do so, and anything which would permanently deprive him of that right of property would be the subject of an action if it were not authorized by Act of Parliament." Baron MARTIN said :—" Although he had not the soil of the bed of the river, he had the easement or right or privilege (by whatever name it may be called) of the flow of the River Thames in its natural channel up to his garden wall. . . . And if any one had done an act injurious to the right to the flow of the water, he would have had a legal right of action against him." And Lord CAIRNS said :—" The property in this case was what is commonly called riparian property. The meaning of that is that it had a water frontage. The meaning of its having a water frontage was this, that it had a right to the undisturbed flow of the river which passed along the whole frontage of the property in the form in which it had been accustomed to pass. That being the state of things, this water frontage with these rights was taken for the purposes of the Act. Beyond all doubt the water-right was a property belonging to the plaintiff for which compensation was to be made."

So also Lord PENZANCE in *The Metropolitan Board of Works* v. *McCarthy* :—" The immediate contiguity to a highway, commonly called frontage, is a well-known and powerful element in the value of all lands in populous districts. When frontage to a high road does not exist, propinquity and easy access to a high road are equally undoubted elements of value in such districts, distinguishing lands which have them from those which have them not. If, then, the lands of any owner have a special value by reason of their proximity to any particular highway, surely that owner will suffer special damage in respect of these lands beyond that suffered by the general public if the benefits of that proximity are withdrawn by the highway being obstructed. And if so, the owner of such lands appears to me to fall within the rule under which an action is maintainable, though the right interfered with is a public one."

And in *Lyon* v. *Fishmongers' Company* (L. R., 1 App. Cas. 662), Lord CAIRNS said :—" Unquestionably the owner of a wharf on the river bank has, like every other subject of the realm, the right of navigating the river as one of the public. This, however, is not a right coming to him *qua* owner or occupier of any lands on the bank, nor is it a right which *per se* he enjoys in a manner different from any other member of the public. But when this right of navigation is connected with exclusive access to and from a particular wharf, it assumes a very different character. It ceases to be a right held in common with the rest of the public, for other members of the public have no access to or from the river at the particular place; and it becomes a form of enjoyment of the land, and of the river in connection with the land, the disturbance of which may be vindicated in damages by an action or restrained by an injunction. It is, as was decided in the cases to which I have referred (*Duke of Buccleuch* v. *The Metropolitan Board of Works; The Metropolitan Board of Works* v. *McCarthy*), a portion of the valuable enjoyment of the land, and any work which takes it away, is held to be an 'injurious affecting' of the land,—that is to say, the occasioning to the land of an 'injuria' or an infringement of right. The taking away of river frontage of a wharf, or the raising of an impediment along the frontage, interrupting the access between the wharf and the river, may be an injury to the public right of navigation; but it is not the less an injury to the owner of the wharf which, in the absence of any Parliamentary authority, would be compensated by damages or altogether prevented. It appears to me impossible to say that a right of enjoyment of land on the bank of a navigable river which is thus valuable and as to which a landowner can thus protect himself against disturbance, is otherwise than a right or claim to which the owner of land on the bank of the river is by law entitled within the meaning of such a saving clause as that which I have read."

From the foregoing cases, it would appear that, under the English Statutes, the following four principles have been established:—

(1.) The damage must be such as, if caused by a private person, might have formed the subject of an action.

(2.) It must be a damage affecting the land of the claimant, independent of any particular trade which may have been carried on upon it.

(3.) It must be a special damage, peculiarly affecting the claimant as distinguished from the rest of the world.

(4.) It must be a damage caused by and during the construction of the works, and not by their subsequent use.

These propositions may now be said to be settled law in England, though the first, second, and fourth were not established without opposition. The second rule in particular was thought to be a hard one, and the Indian Legislature appears to have intended to lay down a more liberal principle. " Regarding compensation for the loss of earnings," said Mr. Strachey, "the Bill dealt decidedly more liberally with private interests than the English law; for mere obstruction or inconvenience to trade was not now regarded by the English law as supporting a claim for compensation." It must be borne in mind, however, that the wording of the English Statutes is very different from the Indian Act; and although the principles laid down in England, when independent of the wording of the Statutes, may usefully be followed in this country, still when on the other hand, they depend on the particular wording of the English Statute, care must be taken in applying them to cases under the Indian Act. For instance, by the English Statute *any one whose land is injuriously affected* by the acquisition can claim compensation; by the Indian Act, in order to be entitled to compensation, a person must have or claim to have an *interest in the land which is acquired*. It is true that the definition of land is very wide and includes any benefit arising therefrom, such as an easement or a right of frontage. But still it is submitted that in order to recover consequential damages, say on account of loss of earnings, the injury complained of must be shown to be closely connected with the acquisition of the land actually taken, and special damage or individual particular loss arising out of that connection must be proved. It is doubtful, indeed, whether even under the Indian Act compensation could have been recovered in *Richet's* case. In that case compensation was refused—*first*, because the evidence did not disclose any damage which, if caused by a private person, would have been actionable; and *secondly*, because it was not shown that any permanent damage had been caused to the plaintiff's premises. By the Indian Act, the latter would not be a necessary condition, but it would have been necessary to show that there had been an infringement of some special benefit arising out of the land actually acquired; while on the first ground the claim would have been barred by s. 25, cl. 3.

As regards certain modes in which an indigo factory was held to be injuriously affected by reason of the acquisition of certain of its lands, see *Taylor* v. *The Collector of Purneah*, I. L. R., 14 Cal. 423.

It will be observed that by the Indian Act compensation may be granted not only for injury to *land*, but also for injury to *move-*

able property (see *Knock's case, ante*) as well as to earnings. Both in England and in India it has been held that all damage which can be foreseen and is capable of being estimated at the time of awarding compensation, should be claimed and assessed once for all — *Croft* v. *London and North-Western Railway Company*, 32 L. J., Q. B. 113. In a subsequent suit for compensation, whether the damage could reasonably have been foreseen at the time of the acquisition, is a question of fact to be determined by the Court — *Tapidas Govindbhai* v. *The B. B. and C. I. Railway Company*, 6 Bom. Rep., A. C. J. 116.

(4.) *Expenses of removal.*

Residence would probably be held to include a place of business.

<small>Matters to be neglected in determining compensation.</small> 25. But the Judge or assessors shall not take into consideration—

First, the degree of urgency which has led to the acquisition:

Secondly, any disinclination of the person interested to part with the land acquired:

Thirdly, any damage sustained by him which, if caused by a private person, would not render such person liable to a suit:

Fourthly, any damage which, after the time of awarding compensation, is likely to be caused by or in consequence of the use to which the land acquired will be put:

Fifthly, any increase to the value of the land acquired likely to accrue from the use to which it will be put when acquired:

Sixthly, any increase to the value of the other land of the person interested, likely to accrue from the use to which the land acquired will be put; or

Seventhly, any outlay or improvements on such land made, commenced or effected, with the intention of enhancing the compensation to be awarded therefor under this Act.

(1.) *The urgency of the acquisition.*

By s. 24, cl. 1, the market-value of the property is to be awarded,—that is, the price which an ordinary purchaser might be expected to pay for it. The Court is not to take into consideration any special value it may possess for the Government or for the purposes of the acquisition, nor, on the other hand, any special value it may possess for the owner (cl. 2).

(2.) *The disinclination of the owner to sell.*

This clause forbids the award of a 'fancy' price. The compulsory nature of the transaction is compensated by the additional allowance under s. 42. Further, a personal feeling or an unwillingness to sell is too vague and inappreciable an element in the transaction to be correctly valued in money. No compensation can be given for destroying a picturesque effect, or for interfering with a sentimental association, such as that attached to a ruin. Nor for annoyance to the amenities of a claimant's property—*Penny* v. *South-Eastern Railway Company*, 26 L. J., Q. B. 225; nor for mere personal inconvenience—*Caledonian Railway Company* v. *Ogilvy*, 2 Macq. 229. See also *Stebbing* v. *Metropolitan Board of Works*, L. R., 6 Q. B. 37.

In *The Collector of Poonah* v. *Kashinath Khasgiwala*, I. L. R., 10 Bom. 585, it was held that the grievance that offerings to idols in a temple would by reason of the acquisition of certain land have to be carried through the public street and would thereby lose their religious efficacy, was too sentimental to admit of any compensation being awarded for it. And, further, that no compensation could be awarded for the mere possibility of treasure-trove in the land.

(3.) *Damage which, if caused by a private person, would not be actionable.*

That is, the injury for which compensation is claimed must be an infringement of some right—not a mere *damnum absque injuriâ*. *Ex damno sine injuria non oritur actio*. This is one of the principles which the English Courts have adopted in awarding compensation. See the cases cited under s. 24, cl. (3), and in particular, *Ricket* v. *Metropolitan Railway Company*; *Metropolitan Board of Works* v. *McCarthy*; and *Duke of Buccleuch* v. *Metropolitan Board of Works*. See also *The New River Company* v. *Johnson* (29 L. J., M. C. 93), in which it was held that the plaintiff was not entitled to compensation, because the company, in the exercise of its statutory powers, constructed some underground works on their own land which drew off the water from plaintiff's well. So, where the tenant of a public-house claimed compensation for the loss of profits he had sustained by reason of a railway company having pulled down the adjoining houses, it was held that he was not entitled to compensation; for if any private person had purchased and pulled down the adjoining property, no action would have lain against him—*Reg.* v. *Vaughan*, L. R., 4 Q. B. 190; 38 L. J., M. C. 49. So, where by the obstruction of a public thoroughfare, injury was occasioned to the plaintiff's business—*Herring* v. *Metropolitan Board of Works*, 34 L. J., M. C. 224. See also Lord Campbell's remarks in *Penny* v. *South-Eastern Railway Company*, 26 L. J., Q. B. 225; and *Rhodes* v. *Airedale Drainage Commissioners*, L. R., 1 C. P. C. 380, 402.

"The object of this provision is to exclude vexatious claims which might be made on account of trifling inconveniences caused during the progress of the works." *Speech of Mr. Strachey.*

As regards the infringement of rights naturally incident to the possession and ownership of land, see Addison on Torts, chap. 2.

(4.) *Prospective damage likely to be caused by, or in consequence of, the use to which the land acquired will be put.*

This clause is not very clearly worded, but there can be no great doubt as to its meaning. By s. 6, the purpose for which the land is needed must be published in the declaration, and the object of such publication is not only to bear out the declaration that the land is needed for a public purpose, but also to apprise the persons interested of the nature of that purpose in order that they may consider how the proposed acquisition will affect their other property or their earnings, and prefer their claims accordingly. The work for which the land is acquired may deprive a person interested of an easement or of a water frontage (as in the *Duke of Buccleuch's* case), and it can never have been intended that such damage should not be taken into account. Any damage can and must be taken into account which can be clearly foreseen as arising out of the purpose for which the land is declared to be needed and acquired—*Tapidas Govindbhai* v. *The B. B. & C. I. Railway Co.*, 6 Bom. Rep., A. C. J. 116. The clause under consideration seems to have reference to prospective and future damages that cannot be foreseen. The leading case on the subject is that of *Lee* v. *Milner* (2 M. & W. 824), in which it was held, that "the jury have no right to assess prospective damages except after an *example* of damage has actually occurred. The cause of injury must exist in some work of the company which is then already done, and that work must be in such a state as to be incapable of further

alteration so as to obviate the damage." As Mr. Strachey said:—
"Any person interested in the property might at any future
time recover by suit compensation for any damage which could not
be foreseen when the property was taken. All that was intended
was that, in fixing the value at the time of taking the property, the
official valuers should not take into consideration purely specula-
tive or imaginary damages."

In *Hummersmith and City Railway Company* v. *Brand* (L. R.
4 H. L., Eng. and Ir. App. 171), it was held that compensation
could only be given under the Land Clauses Consolidation Act
for damage done in the construction of the works, and not for
damage done afterwards when the works are completed and in
the exercise of the statutory powers. Accordingly, compensation
was refused which had been claimed on the ground of the vibration
caused by the passing of trains whereby the plaintiff's property
was depreciated. So in regard to the noise and smoke caused by
the passing of trains—*City of Glasgow Railway Company* v. *Hunter*,
L. R., 2 H. L. Sc. 78. But, although compensation may not be
granted to a person annoyed by the smoke and vibration caused
by trains passing along a railway constructed under an Act of
Parliament when no part of his land has been taken, compensation
may be given for deterioration in the value of his property
occasioned in a similar manner when a part of his land has been
taken for the construction of the work—*Duke of Buccleuch* v.
Metropolitan Board of Works, L. R., 5 H. L. 418.

(5.) *Increase to the value of the land acquired from the use to
which it will be put.*

In *Stebbing* v. *Metropolitan Board of Works* (L. R., 6 Q. B. 37),
it was held that a churchyard which had been closed and was
practically valueless could not be assessed at the value it would
have for the purpose for which it was taken under the Act. It may
happen that the declaration of the purpose for which the land is
to be acquired, as for instance, the construction of a dock, may
have the effect of enhancing the value of all property in the
neighbourhood, including that of the land to be acquired. The
effect of this clause would seem to be that such enhanced value
is not to be taken into consideration in determining the compensation; but this view is somewhat inconsistent with s. 24, cl. (1).

(6.) *Increase to the value of other land from the use to which the
land acquired will be put.*

In *Eagle* v. *Charing Cross Railway Company* (L. R., 2 C. P. 638), it was held that the fact that, notwithstanding the diminution of light, the saleable value of the plaintiff's interest in the premises had not been diminished (the value of the property in the neighbourhood generally having become greatly enhanced by reason of the company's works) was no answer to the claim for compensation. So in *Senior* v. *Metropolitan Railway Company* (32 L. J., Exch. 225) it was held, that the company had no right to set off an ultimate possible benefit accruing to the premises of the person interested, or to the neighbourhood in consequence of the construction of the railroad against the present pecuniary loss caused by the execution of the work.

The construction of railways, roads and canals naturally increases the value of all lands in the neighbourhood, and not merely the land of the person through whose estate they may pass; and there is no reason why such a person should be deprived of a benefit which other proprietors in the neighbourhood will enjoy. Moreover, there are practical difficulties in estimating with any approach to certainty the extent to which the value of a property will be increased by the execution of a projected work.

(7.) *Improvements effected with the intention of enhancing the compensation.*

So, in England, where the owner of property, after a notice to treat had been served on him, entered into an agreement with a person who had for several years occupied part of the property as a weekly tenant for a lease of the same to him for a term of three years, it was held that the tenant was not entitled to compensation in respect of the interest created by such agreement—*In re Marylebone (Stingo Lane) Improvement Act. Ex parte Edwards*, L. R., 12 Eq. 389. And where a landowner built on land after a notice to treat, it was held that he could not compel the company to take the house under s. 92. *Littler* v. *Rhyl Improvement Commissioners*, W. N. (1878), p. 219.

26. Where the person interested has made a claim to compensation, pursuant to any notice mentioned in section nine or in section nineteen, the amount awarded to him shall not exceed the amount so claimed, or be less than the amount tendered by the Collector under section eleven.

Rules as to amount of compensation.

Where the person interested has refused to make such claim, or has omitted without sufficient reason (to be allowed by the Judge) to make such claim, the amount awarded may be less than, and shall in no case exceed, the amount so tendered.

Where the person interested has omitted for a sufficient reason (to be allowed by the Judge) to make such claim, the amount awarded to him shall not be less than, and may exceed, the amount so tendered.

The provisions of this and the two preceding sections shall be read to every assessor, in a language which he understands, before he gives his opinion as to the amount of compensation to be awarded under this Act.

> The rules laid down in this section limit the amount of compensation in three cases, *viz.*:—
>
> (a) *Where the person interested has made a claim*—in which case the amount awarded shall not exceed the claim, or be less than the amount tendered. This is the ordinary rule of the Civil Courts.
>
> (b) *Where the person interested has refused to make a claim, or omitted to do so without sufficient reason.* In this case, the amount awarded may be less than, and shall in no case exceed, the amount tendered.
>
> (c) *Where the Judge thinks there was sufficient cause for such omission*—in which case the amount awarded shall not be less than, and may exceed, the amount tendered.

Record of assessor's opinion.

27. The opinion of each assessor shall be given orally and shall be recorded in writing by the Judge.

> There is no objection to the Judge and assessors consulting together before the latter deliver their opinions, and in practice such consultation is desirable.

28. In case of a difference of opinion between the Judge and the assessors or any of them upon a question of law or practice or usage

Difference on questions of law.

having the force of law, the opinion of the Judge shall prevail, and there shall be no appeal therefrom.

> The point as to whether the damage would be actionable if caused by a private person (s. 25, cl. 3) would be a question of law, on which the opinion of the Judge would prevail; and so generally, as to the *right* to compensation. See note to s. 21.
>
> *And there shall be no appeal therefrom.*—That is, if ultimately they agree as to the amount of compensation. But if, on the other hand, they ultimately differ as to the amount of compensation, an appeal will lie under s. 35, and in that appeal all questions decided by the lower Court, whether the opinion of the assessors coincided with that of the Judge or not, would be open to the parties in the appellate Court—*Secretary of State for India in Council* v. *Sham Bahadoor*, I. L. R., 10 Cal. 769.

29. In case the Judge and one or both of the assessors agree as to the amount of compensation, their decision thereon shall be final.

Agreement as to amount of compensation.

> "Looking at s. 24, the 'amount of compensation' must be taken to mean, not the different matters that are to be taken into consideration separately, but the whole compensation." Accordingly, where the Judge differed wholly from one assessor and differed from the other assessor in the amounts awarded for the different items, but stated that he would not express a dissentient opinion, and agreed with him in the total amount awarded, it was held that there was not such a difference of opinion between the Judge and assessors as entitled the parties to appeal under s. 35—*Ananda Krishna Bose* v. *Verner*, 13 B. L. R. 300; 22 W. R. 350. The High Court, nevertheless, has the power of superintendence over the Courts established by this Act under s. 15 of 24 & 25 Vict., cap. 104. And, therefore, where the Collector tendered compensation in respect of two pieces of land, one of which was above and the other below high-water mark in a tidal navigable river and made an offer for each separately, it was held that the Judge and assessors had no power to award the whole sum tendered by the Collector as compensation for the land above high-water mark, but they should have determined what was a proper compensation for each description of land—*In the matter of the Petition of Abdool Ali*, 15 B. L. R. 197; 23 W. R. 73. But where the Judge and

one of the assessors differed from the Collector, and from each other as to the relative value of a piece of land and a building standing upon it, but agreed with each other and with the Collector as to the total amount of compensation to be awarded for both, it was held that, looking at the definition of 'land' in s. 3, the award was final, and the Calcutta High Court, distinguishing the case from that of Abdool Ali, declined to interfere. *In the matter of Tulsee Das Sen and another*, Rule 1511 of 1885, decided on 1st February 1886.

30. In case of difference of opinion between the Judge and both of the assessors as to the amount of compensation, the decision of the Judge shall prevail, subject to the appeal allowed under section thirty-five.

Difference as to amount of compensation.

It is immaterial whether or not the assessors agree with one another—*Heysham* v. *Bholanath Mullick; Bholanath Mullick* v. *Heysham*, 11 B. L. R. 230.

31. Every assessor appointed under this Act, not being an officer of Government, shall receive such fee for his services as the Judge shall direct, provided that such fee shall not exceed five hundred rupees.

Assessors' fees.

Such fee shall be deemed to be costs in the proceeding.

That is, the fee of *each* assessor may be fixed at any sum not exceeding Rs. 500.

32. The costs of all proceedings taken under this Part by order of the Court shall, in the first instance, be paid by the Collector.

Costs of proceedings taken by order of Court.

This section does not refer to costs of apportionment proceedings under Part IV. But, in order to expedite such proceedings, the costs are usually advanced in the first instance by the Collector.

33. Where the amount awarded does not exceed the sum tendered by the Collector, the costs of all proceedings under this Part shall be paid by the person interested.

Party to pay costs.

Where the amount awarded exceeds the sum so tendered, such costs shall be paid by the Collector.

The rule here laid down is, of course, subject to special arrangement, as where the Court grants a postponement on an understanding that one or other party pay the costs thereof. The rule does not apply to costs incurred in trying questions of apportionment as between the persons interested under Part IV of the Act ; and it is open to question whether it should apply to costs incurred under s. 15, cl. 5, in trying questions of title or right.

By the person interested.—By the next section the Court is empowered to decide by what particular person or persons and in what proportions the costs are to be paid.

34. Every award made under this Part shall be in writing signed by the Judge and the assessor or assessors concurring therein, and shall specify the amount awarded under the first clause of section twenty-four, and also the amounts (if any) respectively awarded under the second, third and fourth clauses of the same section, together with the grounds of awarding each of the said amounts.

<small>Awards to be in writing.</small>

It shall also state the amount of costs incurred in the proceedings under this Part, and by what persons and in what proportions they are to be paid.

<small>Award to state amount of costs.</small>

The costs (if any) payable by the person interested and not deducted under section forty-two may be recovered as if they were costs incurred in a suit, and as if the award were the decree therein.

<small>Recovery of costs.</small>

If the Judge differs from both the assessors, the award need not apparently be signed by either of them. The award should specify the amount awarded under each clause of s. 24 separately, together with the grounds on which each of such amounts was awarded. It will operate as the decree in the case, and should contain all that is necessary to be entered in a decree.

There being no stamp-duty on the claim (Court Fees Act, VII of 1870, s. 19, cl. xxii), the costs principally consist of the pleaders' fees, witnesses' expenses, process fees, and the fees (if any) of the assessors. As regards the pleaders' fees, the Calcutta High Court has made the following rule under the Legal Practitioners' Act :—

" In this and the following rules cases under Part III of the Land Acquisition Act of 1870, shall be deemed to be suits, and the fees allowable therein may be calculated either on the amount of compensation decreed in excess of the sum tendered by the Collector, or on any smaller amount which the Court in its discretion may think proper. In the event of the sum tendered by the Collector being decreed, pleaders' fees may be awarded to Government on the difference between that sum and the sum claimed, or on any smaller amount which the Court in its discretion may think proper: Provided that, in any case in which the remuneration under the above rules shall, in the opinion of the Judge, prove to be insufficient, or in any case not provided for, he shall be at liberty to allow pleaders' fees, as in miscellaneous cases under Rule 8."

There is no appeal against the order in the award as to costs. " The Judge is to determine the amount of costs incurred by either party in the same way as it is done in suits by the taxing officer." —*Per* COUCH, C. J., *Bamasoonderee Dossee* v. *Verner*, 13 B. L. R. 189 ; 22 W. R. 136.

The last clause of the section refers to a case in which the costs may exceed the amount awarded, or may be adjudged to be payable by a person to whom no part of the compensation has been awarded.

The award is not chargeable with stamp-duty, and any party claiming under it is entitled to a copy free of charge (s. 57).

35. If the Judge differs from both the assessors as to the amount of compensation, he shall pronounce his decision, and the Collector or the person interested (as the case may be) may appeal therefrom to the Court of the District Judge, unless the Judge whose decision is appealed from is the District Judge, or unless the amount which the Judge proposes to award exceeds five thousand rupees, in either of which cases the appeal shall lie to the High Court.

Appeal from Judge's decision as to compensation.

Every appeal under this section shall be presented within the time and in manner provided by the Code of Civil Procedure for regular appeals in suits.

> This section refers to cases in which the Judge differs from both assessors as to the amount of compensation under s. 30.
>
> In Calcutta it has been held that an appeal from the decision of a special Judge appointed under s. 3, within the local limits of the original jurisdiction of the High Court, will lie to that Court as the ordinary appellate Court of the district, even though the amount of compensation may not exceed Rs. 5,000.—*Bamasoonderee Dossee* v. *Verner*, 13 B. L. R. 189 ; 22 W. R. 136. But contra, see *Aroomachella Gramany* v. *Velliappa Gramany*, 8 Mad. Rep. 103. As to the right of appeal on questions of law or title, see the remarks of Mr. (now Justice) FIELD in *Raja Nilmony Singh* v. *Ram Bandhu Roy*, 3 C. L. R. 211 :—"It then follows that the Judge, in order to decide the proportions in which the persons interested are entitled to share in the amount of compensation, has jurisdiction to decide any question respecting the title to the land, or any rights thereto or interests therein, which may arise between or among two or more persons making conflicting claims in respect thereof (cl. 5, s. 15); that in deciding this question he is to be guided by the usual procedure of the Civil Courts; and that the person or persons to whom his decision may be adverse have the same right of appeal to the superior tribunals which is enjoyed by the parties to ordinary civil suits."
>
> Compare the last clause of this section with that of s. 39. The words "by the Code of Civil Procedure" in s. 39 were repealed by Act XII of 1876, and the repeal should have extended to this section. The time within which appeals must be presented is now regulated by the Indian Limitation Act, XV of 1877, Part II. An appeal to a District Judge must be presented within thirty days from the date of the award (Sched. II, Art. 152), and an appeal to the High Court within ninety days (Art. 156). The memorandum of appeal is not exempted from the usual Court-fee.

Provisions of Code of Civil Procedure made applicable.

36. The following provisions of the Code of Civil Procedure—

(*a*) as to adding parties,

(*b*) as to adjournment,

(*c*) as to death, marriage, and bankruptcy or insolvency of parties,

(*d*) as to summoning witnesses and their attendance,

(*e*) as to examination of parties and witnesses,

(*f*) as to production of documents, and

(*g*) as to commissions to examine absent witnesses and to make local enquiries,

shall apply, so far as may be, to proceedings before the Court.

(*a.*) *As to adding parties*, see s. 32, C. C. P. Parties added on or before the first hearing should be allowed an opportunity to file a claim (s. 26) and nominate an assessor.

(*b.*) *As to adjournment*, see ss. 156—158, C. C. P.

(*c.*) *As to death, marriage, &c.*, see ss. 361—372, C. C. P.

(*d.*) *As to summoning witnesses, &c.*, see ss. 159—178, C. C. P.

(*e.*) *As to examination of parties*, see ss. 117—120; *and of witnesses*, ss. 181—193, C. C. P.

(*f.*) *As to production of documents*, see ss. 138—145, C. C. P.; but probably the whole of Chap. X would be held to be applicable.

(*g.*) *As to commissions to examine witnesses*, see ss. 383—391; *and for local investigations*, ss. 392—393, C. C. P.

A proceeding under this Part should, as far as possible, be treated as a suit in which the various claimants are plaintiffs and the Collector the defendant.

PART IV.

APPORTIONMENT OF COMPENSATION.

37. Where there are several persons interested, if such persons agree in the apportionment of the compensation, the particulars of such apportionment shall be specified in the award, and as between such persons the award shall be conclusive evidence of the correctness of the apportionment.

Particulars of apportionment to be specified.

The award spoken of in this section may be either that made by the Collector under s. 14, or that made by the Court under s. 34.

"*As between such persons.*"—But it will not, of course, bind persons who are not before the Collector or the Court making the award—*Hurmutjan Bibi* v. *Padma Lochan Das*, I. L. R., 12 Cal. 33.

38. When the amount of compensation has been settled under section fourteen, if any dispute arises as to the apportionment of the same or any part thereof, the Collector shall refer such dispute to the decision of the Court.

Dispute as to apportionment.

The Collector has no power to decide disputes as to apportionment.

There appears to be an important distinction between a reference under this section, and a reference under s. 15, cl. (5), where a question arises between two or more claimants respecting the title to the land or any rights thereto or interests therein. A reference under this section presupposes that the rights and interests of the various claimants are undisputed, but that they cannot agree amongst themselves as to the apportionment of the compensation. In such a case, an award may be made, but the money is not payable pending the dispute as to the apportionment. In the case of a reference under s. 15, no award can be made until the question as to title has been decided.

The costs in a reference under this section should probably be borne by the persons interested. Compare Bengal Act III of 1876, s. 23.

39. When the amount of compensation has been settled by the Court, and there is any dispute as to the apportionment thereof, or when a reference to the Court has been made under section thirty-eight, the Judge sitting alone shall decide the proportions in which the persons interested are entitled to share in such amount.

Determination of proportions.

An appeal shall lie from such decision to the High Court, unless the Judge whose decision is appealed from is not the

District Judge, in which case the appeal shall lie in the first instance to the District Judge.

Every appeal under this section shall be presented within the time and in manner provided for regular appeals in suits.

> The amount of compensation having been settled either by the Collector under Part II, or by the Judge and assessors under Part III of the Act, this section prescribes that the Judge sitting alone shall decide any dispute that may arise as to the apportionment of the money. Such disputes often involve questions of right and title: by this section, therefore, all such questions referred to the Court under s. 15, cl. (5), are to be tried by the Judge in the proceedings under this Act, and not left, as formerly, to be decided in a separate suit. This change in the law was not at first recognized by the Courts, as appears from the remarks made in *Dwarka Singh* v. *E. Solano*, 22 W. R. 38; *Gour Ram Chunder* v. *Sonatun Das*, 25 W. R. 320; *In the matter of the Petition of Abdool Ali*, 15 B. L. R. 197; 23 W. R. 73. But the question has now been set at rest by the decisions in the cases of *Raja Nilmoni Singh Deo* v. *Rambandhu Roy*, I. L. R., 4 Cal. 757; 7 *ibid*, 388; S. C. 3 C. L. R. 211, and 10 C. L. R. 393; and *Nobodeep Chunder Chowdhry* v. *Brojendro Lall Roy and others*, I. L. R., 7 Cal. 406. In the latter case, PONTIFEX, J., said:—"We think it right to say that under s. 39 it is the duty of the Judge, in apportioning the compensation-money which he is directed to apportion, to decide the question of title between all persons claiming a share of the money." And the decision of the question in these proceedings, though open to appeal, cannot be contested by any of the parties to it in a regular suit.—*Raja Nilmoni Singh* v. *Rambandhu Roy*, *ante*.

> The question of apportionment may be decided in the same proceedings in which the amount of compensation is determined. *The Collector of Poonah* v. *Kasinath Khasgiwala*, I. L. R., 10 Bom. 585. Each party is bound to prove his title to the compensation he claims, and is not entitled to succeed merely because the other party fails to make out his case. (Reg. App. 312 and 313 of 1884, Calcutta High Court, not reported.)

> The following decisions lay down the principles on which the apportionment of the compensation-money should be made between

a zemindar and the various subordinate tenure-holders. The leading case on the subject is that of *Srinath Mookerjee and others* v. *Maharajah Mahtap Chand Bahadoor* (S. D. A. 1860, 326), in which the late Sudder Dewany Adawlut said:—
"The zemindar and the putneedar are entitled to compensation in proportion to the losses they respectively sustain from the appropriation of their lands and to the remission of the rents which they pay respectively to the Government or the zemindar.
. . . . The proper principle we consider to be as follows:— In respect to remission, as the gross rental of the whole putnee is to the gross rent of the land proposed to be taken, so will the entire putnee rent be to the particular portion of the rent to be remitted ; and, with regard to compensation, the principle may most conveniently be stated as follows,—as the gross profit of the putnee is to the profit of the putneedar, so will the gross compensation be to the portion of the compensation the putneedar is entitled to recover. These formulæ are of universal application, and will enable any one hereafter to adjust the remission and compensation between zemindar and putneedar without difficulty in any case that may arise." So in *Gordon, Stuart & Co.* v. *Maharajah Mahtap Chand Bahadoor* (Marsh. 490), it was held that where lands are taken compulsorily, the principle upon which the amount of compensation is divisible amongst the zemindar and the holders of several subordinate tenures, is to ascertain the value of the interest of each holder of a tenure and to give him a sum equivalent to the purchase-money of such interest. But the principle in the Sudder Dewany Adawlut case is not applicable to the case of several putnees subordinate to one another, where the land is taken from the holder of the last tenure and where the grantors of the several intermediate tenures have received a sum of money as a bonus for the grant—*Maharajah Mahtap Chand Bahadoor* v. *Bengal Coal Company and others,* 10 W. R. 391. In another case, where by the calculation of the plaintiff (a dur-putneedar) a more favourable result was secured to the zemindar than that for which he himself contended, it was held to be unnecessary to go into the proper principle on which the compensation should be apportioned—*Bengal Coal Company* v. *Maharajah Mahtap Chand Bahadoor,* 12 W. R. 340. A putneedar is entitled to compensation, though there may be no agreement to that effect—*Joykissen Mookerjee* v. *Reazoonissa Beebee,*

4 W. R. 40. The party *primâ facie* entitled to the compensation is the proprietor; any party claiming against him by virtue of a right derived from him (*e. g.*, mokurrareedar) is bound to prove the right he pleads.—*Issur Chunder Banerjee* v. *Sattyo Dyal Banerjee*, 12 W. R. 270.

In a suit between a putneedar and a zemindar for apportionment of compensation-money in deposit with the Collector under Act VI of 1857, COUCH, C. J., said:—" The compensation ought to be apportioned between the parties according to the value of the interest which each of them parts with. The zemindar has a right to the fixed rent, and the loss he sustains is of so much of his rent. Any other possible injury, such as the chance of the putneedar throwing up the land, and its being diminished in value by what has been taken by Government and still remaining, as it did, liable to pay the same revenue, is, we think, not appreciable and cannot be taken into account. If there is no abatement of the rent and the putneedar continues liable to pay to the zemindar the same rent as he had to pay before, there would be nothing for which the zemindar ought to receive compensation. He would be in the same position as before, except with reference, as we have said, to the possibility of a loss which is scarcely appreciable. But the proper mode of settling the rights of the parties is to give to the putneedar an abatement of his rent in proportion to the quantity of land which has been taken from him. It is not fair that he should be liable to pay the same rent when a part of the land has been taken away. The decision of the Judge that the plaintiff is entitled to an abatement of the rent is correct, and is in accordance with the principle laid down in the case of the Maharajah of Burdwan. This being so, the zemindar ought to be compensated for the loss of rent which he sustains, and the money ought to be divided between the parties accordingly. The putneedar's getting an abatement of his rent is to be taken into account as partly the way in which he is compensated for the loss of the land."—*Raye Kissory Dassee* v. *Nilcant Day*, 20 W. R. 370.

On the other hand, see the remarks of GARTH, C. J., in *Godadhar Dass* v. *Dhunpat Sing*, I. L. R., 7 Cal. 589:—" As regards the zemindar, it is a mistake to suppose that his interest in the land is confined entirely to the rent which he receives from the putneedar. He is the owner of it under the Government; and in the event of the putnee coming to an end by sale, forfeiture or otherwise, the property would revert to the zemindar, who might deal with it as he pleased in its improved state; and although in some cases the chances of the putnee coming to an end may be more or less remote, there is no doubt that in all cases the zemindar is entitled to some compensation (small though it be) for the loss of his rights. At any rate he would generally be entitled to receive as much as the putneedar." In *Banwari Lall Chowdhry* v. *Burnomoyi Dassee* (I. L. R., 14 Cal. 749), the District Judge, acting on the above principle, had decreed that the compensation should be divided equally between the zemindar and the putneedar, and the Court said:—"It seems to us that no general principle can be laid down applicable to every case as between zemindar and putneedar. The apportionment between the zemindar and the putneedar will depend partly on the sum paid as bonus for the putnee and the relation that it bore to the probable value of the property, and partly on the amount of rent payable to the zemindar, and also the actual proceeds from the cultivating tenants or under-tenants. It may occasionally happen that the zemindar receives an extremely high bonus, and is content with charging the property with the receipt of a very low rate of rent, or it may be that the bonus is almost nominal and the rent is excessively high, and the zemindar depends not on the bonus and the interest of the amount so paid and invested in some other way, but on the amount paid periodically as rent; and consequently as between parties standing in these relations, it is necessary to consider all these matters before any conclusion can be arrived at as to their rights to any particular compensation." It is open to question, however, whether in any case where the zemindar has granted a putnee or other permanent saleable under-tenure, he ought to be held to be entitled to more than the capitalized value of the rent of the land taken. The receipt of a high bonus is nothing more than the receipt in anticipation of a portion of the rent capitalized. In two cases (Reg. App. 271 and 272 of 1885, Calcutta, not reported) where the land taken had been let in a permanent under-tenure, and no abatement of the rent had been granted, the High Court held that the under-tenant was entitled to the entire compensation.

Where a putneedar has taken the whole amount of the compensation without claiming any abatement of rent, a subsequent purchaser of the putnee is not at liberty to re-open the question and to sue for abatement.—*Peari Mohan Mookerjee* v. *Audhiraj Aftab Chand*, 10 C. L. R. 526.

Where land had been granted for building purposes, the High Court of the N. W. P. held that the grantee was entitled to the bulk of the compensation for the land as well as to that for the buildings, the zemindar having at most a reversionary interest.—*Gur Parshad* v. *Umrao Singh*, 7 N. W. P. Rep. 218.

A ryot with a right of occupancy is entitled to share in the compensation. "The parties who usually suffer most from lands being taken for Government purposes are either the ryots with right of occupancy or the holders, whoever they may be, of the first permanent interest above the occupying ryots. The actual occupier is, of course, turned out by the Government, and if he is a ryot with a right of occupancy, he loses the benefit of that right, besides being driven possibly to find a holding and a home elsewhere; and the holder of the tenure immediately superior to the occupying ryots, whatever the nature of the holding may be, loses the rent of the land taken during the period of his holding. These two classes, therefore, would, generally speaking, be entitled to the larger portion of the compensation."—*Per* GARTH, C. J., in *Godadhar Dass* v. *Dhunput Sing*, ante.

Similarly the Madras High Court said :—No definite rule can be laid down as to the rights of the tenants called "Ulkudi Sukhavasis" or "Payakaris," but they have a qualified interest in the soil, and where their land is taken under the Act, they are clearly entitled to compensation for the loss of their interest. In ascertaining the proportionate interest of the Mirasidar and Ulkudi tenant, allowance must be made for the Mirasidar's reversionary right; and when the rights of the parties are calculated on the basis of the value of the produce, allowance must be made for the expenses of cultivation.—*Appasari Modali* v. *Rangappa Nattan*, I. L. R., 4 Mad. 367.

In a case not reported (Reg. App. 477 of 1885), the Calcutta High Court first deducted the value of the rent at 15 years' purchase, and awarded it to the landlord or the ryot with right of occupancy according as there was or was not an abatement of the rent, dividing the balance of the compensation between them.

In *Bhageeruth Moodee* v. *Rajah Jabar Jummah Khan* (18 W. R. 91), it was held that, as under Regulation XXIX of 1814, the zemindar retains an interest in ghatwalli lands, he is entitled to share in the compensation, and in that case he was allowed a one-fourth share. But in a subsequent case it was held, that neither the zemindar nor the under-tenants of the ghatwal could claim a share, but that the compensation-money carried with it all the incidents of the original ghatwalli tenure, and the ghatwal for the time being was entitled only to the interest accruing therefrom during his lifetime.—*Ram Chunder Singh* v. *Jabar Jummah Khan*, 14 B. L. R., App. 7.

Where the land taken was an accretion to a *mourusi* and *muharrari* tenure, it was held that, in the absence of special circumstances, the rent of the accreted land must be taken to be proportionate to that of the original tenure, and that the landlord was entitled to the value of such rent *plus* 15 per cent., the balance of the compensation being given to the tenant.—*Chooramoni Dey* v. *Howrah Mills Co., Ld.*, I. L. R., 11 Cal. 696.

Abatement of rent.—In *Gordon, Stuart & Co.* v. *Maharajah Mahtab Chand Bahadoor and others* (Marsh. 490), it was held that abatement of rent could not be claimed in a suit to recover compensation under the former procedure, such a claim being cognizable only in a suit under Act X of 1859, s. 18. But such a claim may be made by way of set-off in a suit for arrears of rent—*Deen Dyall Lall* v. *Mussamut Thukroo Koonwar*, 6 W. R., Act X, Rul. 24 ; even though the pottah may not provide for a remission of the kind, and the superior holder has not obtained a similar benefit from the zemindar—*Mohesh Chunder Dutt* v. *Gungamoney Dossee and others*, 2 Hay 495. But the abatement claimed must be reckoned with reference not to the gross amount of compensation, but to the proportion which passes into the hands of the superior holder.—*Maharajah Dheraj Mahtab Chand Bahadoor* v. *Chittro Coomaree Bibee*, 16 W. R. 201.

Under the present law, the practice is to grant abatement of rent in the same proceedings in which the compensation is apportioned. Indeed, in many cases, a share of the compensation can only be allowed to the superior tenure-holders on the condition of an abatement of the rent. So in regard to the capitalized Government revenue which is often claimed as belonging to the zemindar. A little consideration will show that the capitalized value of the Government revenue is only a part of the total compensation and must be treated as such ; and, when there are permanent under-tenures, the zemindar is not entitled to that or any other part of the compensation, unless he agrees to make a corresponding reduction in the rent. The Judge "will do wisely to make the parties come to some arrangement as to the abatement."—*Godadhar Dass* v. *Dhunput Sing, ante.*

It was ruled by the Madras High Court that a Judge appointed under s. 3 to perform the functions of a Judge under the Act within the local limits of the ordinary original jurisdiction of the High Court has no power to award costs under this section. "The jurisdiction being of a special nature and exercised under a special enactment, must be strictly confined within the limits given by the statute."—*Ramenjem Naidoo* v. *Rangiah Naidoo,* 8 Mad. H. C. 192.

Appeal.—By s. 8 of the Civil Courts Act XII of 1887, an Additional Judge exercises the same powers as a District Judge, and by s. 20 appeals from his decrees or orders lie to the High Court. The section in question runs as follows :—

"Save as otherwise provided by any enactment for the time being in force, an appeal from a decree or order of a District Judge or Additional Judge shall lie to the High Court.

An appeal shall not lie to the High Court from a decree or order of an Additional Judge in any case in which, if the decree or order had been made by the District Judge, an appeal would not lie to that Court."

In Regular Appeal No. 312 of 1886, decided by the Calcutta High Court on 13th July 1887 but not reported, an objection was taken that under this section an appeal from the decision of an Additional Judge specially appointed under s. 3 to perform the functions of a Judge under this Act lay to the District Judge; but it was held that on the same principle on which the case of *Bamasoonderee Dassee* v. *Verner* (13 B. L. R. 189) was decided, the appeal lay to the High Court. That case, however, was decided when the Bengal Civil Courts Act VI of 1871 was in force, s. 21 of which ran as follows :—

"Appeals from the decrees and orders of District Judges and Additional Judges shall, when such appeals are allowed by law, lie to the High Court."

In *Gobind Lall Seal* v. *Secretary of State for India* (Reg. App. 32 of 1882, Calcutta, not reported), it was doubted whether under this section an appeal will lie in a case where no compensation is awarded, but where merely questions of title are decided. But see *Atri Bai* v. *Arnopoorna Bai,* I. L. R., 9 Cal. 838 ; 12 C. L. R. 409, and *Secretary of State for India in Council* v. *Sham Bahadoor,* I. L. R., 10 Cal. 769. The question as to whether or not there is any appeal from the decision of the Court upon a reference under s. 15, cl, (5) appears to be a *casus omissus* in the Act.

PART V.

PAYMENT.

40. Payment of the compensation shall be made by the Collector according to the award to the persons named therein, or, in the case of an appeal under section thirty-nine, according to the decision on such appeal:

Payment of compensation to whom made.

Provided that nothing herein contained shall affect the liability of any person who may receive the whole or any part of any compensation awarded under this Act, to pay the same to the person lawfully entitled thereto.

Proviso.

This section authorizes and directs the Collector to pay the compensation to the persons named in the award, or according to the decision on appeal. That is to say, the persons so entitled have a right to be paid without further suit, and the Collector is protected in paying them. Similarly under Act VI of 1857, it was ruled that a Collector who after proper enquiry paid the compensation to the person " deemed by him to be in possession as owner " was not liable to be sued by the real owner for the amount.— *Yesoba Dumodhur* v. *Secretary of State for India in Council,* 7 Bom. Rep., O. C. J. 12.

The proviso does not apply to any person who has appeared and been a party to the proceedings under s. 39 of the Act.— On the contrary, any person who is a party to the proceedings under s. 39, is precluded from bringing a regular suit for the whole or any part of the compensation.—*Raja Nilmoni Singh Deo Buhadur* v. *Ram Bandhu Rai,* I. L. R., 7 Cal. 388 ; 10 C. L. R.

393. In that case, their Lordships of the Privy Council said :— "Such a proviso, which appears to have been but a repetition of a provision in a previous Act *in pari materiâ*, is necessary in this, as in almost all Acts of a similar character. It is necessary for the Government, or the persons or company entitled to take the property compulsorily, to deal with those who are in possession or ostensibly the owners ; but it may happen, and frequently does happen, that the real owners, possibly being infants or persons under disability, do not appear and are not dealt with in the first instance; and therefore a provision of this sort is necessary for the purpose of enabling the parties who have a real title to obtain the compensation-money. . . . The proviso applies only to persons whose rights have not been adjudicated upon in pursuance of ss. 38 and 39, and it has not the effect, which it would certainly not be reasonable to attribute to it, of permitting a person whose claim has been adjudicated upon in the manner pointed out by the Act to have that claim re-opened and again heard in another suit. Their Lordships are of opinion that the provisions in this Act for the settling of compensation are intended to be final ; and that the amount and distribution of the compensation having been settled in this case by a competent Court, and the decision not having been appealed against, the settlement is final, and the present suit cannot be maintained." See also the judgment of the High Court, in the same suit, I. L. R., 4 Cal. 757; 3 C. L. R. 210. But the proviso will apply to a person who, though served with notice under s. 19, was no party to the apportionment proceedings under s. 39. The apportionment of the compensation under s. 39 is intended to be a proceeding distinct from that of settling the amount of compensation under the previous provisions of the Act, and any dispute as to the apportionment is only decided as between those persons who are actually before the Court. A separate notice therefore of the apportionment proceedings is requisite to bind any person by those proceedings, and where such a notice has not been served, any party interested although served with notice of proceedings for settling the amount of compensation, cannot be considered a party to the proceedings for apportioning it—*Hurmatjan Bibi* v. *Padma Lochun Das*, I. L. R., 12 Cal. 33. " Where money has been paid into Court by reason of real estate having been taken under the compulsory powers, and remains in Court, it is to be held as

personal estate in the hands of the Court impressed with the trusts of real estate." *Per* STUART, V. C., *In re Stewart's Trusts*, 22 L. J. (N. S.) 369. And therefore where the land had been mortgaged, it was held that the mortgagee had a right to recover the compensation awarded for it—*Viraragava* v. *Krishnasami*, I. L. R., 6 Mad. 844. But a suit to recover the money is not a suit to establish a right to or interest in immoveable property under, s. 16 (*d*) of the Code of Civil Procedure, and it is not necessary therefore that the suit should be instituted in the Court within the local limits of whose jurisdiction the immoveable property is situate.—*Viraragava* v. *Krishnasami*, I. L. R., 6 Mad. 344.

Government took for public purposes a quantity of land which included 4 cottahs leased by M to plaintiff as the site of an iron foundry. Proceedings were duly taken under Act VI of 1857, in which plaintiff did not appear. Five years afterwards he sued to recover compensation for having been turned out of his holding and deprived of the machinery, &c., of his foundry. *Held*, that M as lessor was not answerable for the plaintiff's eviction, and that there was no evidence to show either that plaintiff's property was valued by the arbitrators or at what amount. " We are therefore quite unable to arrive at any judgment as to the aliquot part of the whole compensation and purchase-money which is attributable to the plaintiff's share of the property."—*Minto* v. *Kalee Churn Dass*, 8 W. R. 327.

41. When the amount of the compensation has been settled under section fourteen, if the persons interested shall so desire, the Collector shall, on the making of the said award, pay the amount of such compensation and take possession of the land:

Payment on making award by Collector.

Provided that, in any case where immediate possession is not required, he may allow the occupants (if any) of the land to remain in occupation of the same, upon such terms as he and they may agree on, until possession of the land is required.

This section refers to the time when payment should be made and must be read with s. 42. The section requires the Collector to make payment if he has made an award (which under s. 14 is final as to the amount), *and* if the persons interested consent, that is, if there is no dispute either as to the persons entitled to the compensation or as to the apportionment thereof. But the Collector obviously cannot pay the compensation if he has made a reference to the Court under s. 15 or s. 38, even though he may have made an award. In such a case he is bound to await the result of any appeal that may be preferred against the Court's decision (s. 42). As Mr. Field remarked in *Raja Nilmoni Singh* v. *Ram Bandhu Roy* (3 C. L. R. 217), " the determination of the question of title before payment is made of the amount of compensation obviates the possible mischief of payment to the wrong party, and brings the matter to a speedy conclusion much more satisfactorily than the former plan of the Collector holding the money until the parties had taken their own time to litigate the question of title."

Payment of the compensation is not a condition precedent to taking possession. See s. 16. The proviso should rather have been annexed to that section.

As to the period of limitation for suits for compensation, see Act XV of 1877, sched. II, arts. 17—18. A suit against Government for compensation for land actually acquired must be brought within one year from the date of determining the amount; and a like suit when the acquisition is not completed within one year from the refusal to complete. But see s. 54.

42. In addition to the amount of any compensation awarded under Part II or Part III of this Act, the Collector shall, in consideration of the compulsory nature of the acquisition, pay fifteen per centum on the market-value mentioned in section twenty-four.

Percentage on market-value.

When the amount of such compensation is not paid on taking possession, the Collector shall pay the amount awarded, and the said percentage with interest on such amount and percentage at the rate of six per centum per annum from the time of so taking possession :

Payment with interest.

Provided that the costs, if any, payable to the Collector by the person interested, shall be deducted from such amount and percentage:

Provided that, in cases where the decision of the Court under Part III or Part IV of this Act is liable to appeal, the Collector shall not pay the amount of compensation or the percentage, or any part thereof, until the time for appealing against such decision has expired, and no appeal shall have been presented against such decision, or until any such appeal shall have been disposed of.

Time of payment in appealable cases.

The additional allowance of 15 per cent. is only payable on the *market-value* of the land under cl. 1 of s. 24, and not on any damages that may be awarded under cls. 2, 3 or 4 of that section.

The additional allowance should not form part of the award; it is to be paid over and above the amount awarded.

Interest should be paid up to the date on which the compensation is due. When a reference has been made under s. 38, the Advocate-General of Bengal has expressed the opinion that interest is payable by Government up to the date of decision. The intention of the first proviso appears to be that the costs (if any) should be deducted before interest is calculated.

Formerly, the Collector had to invest the amount in Government securities pending suit or appeal, but this is not now necessary.

Certain rulings under the old law on the subject of payment may be briefly referred to in this place:—In a suit to recover compensation for certain lands taken for roads under Regulation I of 1824, when plaintiff had applied for compensation in the usual course, but after various delays had been refused compensation and referred to the Civil Court after the period of limitation had expired, it was decided that the cause of action arose when the plaintiff was dispossessed from the land and not when compensation was refused, and that he was not entitled to any consideration for his delay in instituting a suit which was the best remedy prescribed by law, and that the mere fact of Government receiving revenue for the estate in which the lands were situated did not prevent the law of limitation from acting in its favour, as it would in the case of any private individual in adverse possession—*James Hills* v. *The Magistrate of Nuddea*, 11 W. R. 1. In *Yesoba Dumodhur* v. *Secretary of State in Council* (7 Bom. Rep., O. C. J. 12), it was held that it was discretionary with the Collector to take advantage of the provisions of s. 29, Act VI of 1857; if after due enquiry he chose to pay to the person deemed by him to be in possession, he was not liable to be sued afterwards by the real owner. When the compensation was kept in deposit and invested under that section, the owner was not entitled to interest beyond what accrued on the Government securities— *Sayad Keramut Ali Mutwalee* v *Rajah Suttochurn Ghosal*, W. R. 1864, 329. In a suit for apportionment of certain compensation-money in deposit with the Collector, it was ruled that the cause of action did not arise until the plaintiff sought to obtain his share of the compensation, and was prevented from doing it by the act of the defendant, who would not join him or enable him to get it from the Collector.—*Raye Kissory Dassea* v. *Nilcunt Dey*, 20 W. R. 370.

PART VI.

Temporary Occupation of Land.

43. Subject to the provisions of Part VII of this Act, whenever it appears to the Local Government that the temporary occupation and use of any waste or arable land are needed for any public purpose, or for a Company, the Local Government may direct the Collector to procure the occupation and use of the same for such term as it shall think fit, not exceeding three years from the commencement of such occupation.

Temporary occupation of waste or arable land.

The Collector shall thereupon give notice in writing to the persons interested in such land of the purpose for which the same is needed, and shall, for the occupation and use thereof for such term as aforesaid, and for the materials (if any) to be taken therefrom, pay to them such compensation, either in a gross sum of money, or by monthly or other periodical payments, as shall be agreed upon in writing between him and such persons respectively.

<small>Difference as to compensation.</small> In case the Collector and the persons interested differ as to the sufficiency of the compensation, the Collector shall refer such difference for the final order of the court.

> Act II of 1861, s. 3, authorized the temporary occupation of any land not more than one hundred yards from the centre line of the road, canal or railway, as marked on the ground, "for taking earth or other materials for making and repairing the road, canal or railway, or for depositing thereon superfluous earth or other materials, or erecting temporary buildings and workshops thereon, and of any land which may be needed for making temporary roads or railways from any public road or any navigable river to the intended line of railway;" and "for the temporary occupation of such land and for any permanent damage done by such occupation and use of the land, including the full value of all clay, stone, gravel, sand, and other materials taken thence," compensation was to be paid to the persons interested therein.
>
> And when the provisions of that section were "inadequate for the purpose of taking ballast or of brick-making or of quarrying for building-stone or limestone," and it was expedient that land should be temporarily occupied beyond such limits, the Government might extend the provisions of that section to any cultivated land within two miles of the line of road, provided it was not being worked or used at the time for the same purpose.
>
> Under the present Act no *local* limits are imposed, but only *waste* or *arable* land can be temporarily occupied, and that only *for a maximum period of three years*. It has been ruled by the Calcutta High Court in *Collector of Gya* v. *Denonath Roy* (not reported) that land actually used as a stone-quarry is not waste land. (30th March 1881.)

<small>Power to enter and take possession.</small> 44. On payment of such compensation, or on executing such agreement, or on making a reference under section forty-three, the Collector may enter upon and take possession of the

land, and use or permit the use thereof in accordance with the terms of the said notice.

And, on the expiration of the term, the Collector shall *Restoration of land taken.* make or tender to the persons interested compensation for the damage (if any) done to the land and not provided for by the agreement, and shall restore the land to the persons interested therein:

Provided that, if the land has become permanently unfit to be used for the purpose for which it was used immediately before the commencement of such term, and if the persons interested shall so require, the Local Government shall proceed under this Act to acquire the land as if it was needed permanently for a public purpose or for a Company.

> Even if payment is made at once in a gross sum, there must apparently, under s. 43, be an *agreement in writing*. The land must be restored on the expiration of the term agreed upon, unless it has become permanently unfit for the purpose for which it was formerly used, and the persons interested insist that the Government shall acquire it permanently.
>
> The Collector must at the same time tender compensation for any further damage done, and if the tender is refused, or there is any dispute as to the amount of damage, the Collector is bound to refer the matter to the Court under the next section.
>
> By Act II of 1861, s. 5, the persons interested could, at any time before agreeing to the compensation or before the order of reference, compel the Government to acquire the land permanently or forego its occupation; under the present Act, however, they cannot do this until the expiration of the temporary occupation, and not then unless the land has been rendered permanently unfit for its former use. In the event of any dispute on the point, the matter must be referred to the Court under s. 45.
>
> If the Government refuse to complete the acquisition, a suit for compensation must be brought within one year from the date of the refusal. Act XV of 1877, Sched. II, Art. 18.

45. In case the Collector and persons interested differ as to the condition of the land at the expiration of the term, or as to any matter connected with the said agreement, the Collector shall refer such difference for the final order of the Court, and on such reference, or on a reference under section forty-three, the Judge sitting alone shall decide the difference referred.

Difference as to condition of land.

As to the condition of the land at the expiration of the term. These words will include both a difference as to the further compensation (if any) to be paid, and a difference as to the permanent unfitness of the land for its former use.

PART VII.

ACQUISITION OF LAND FOR COMPANIES.

46. Subject to such rules as the Governor-General of India in Council may from time to time prescribe in this behalf, the Local Government may authorize any officer of any Company desiring to acquire land for its purposes to exercise the powers conferred by section four.

Company may be authorized to enter and survey.

In every such case section four shall be construed as if, for the words "for such purpose," the words "for the purposes of the Company" were substituted, and section five shall be construed as if, after the words "the officer," the words "of the Company" were inserted.

Construction of sections four and five.

47. The provisions of section six to section forty-five (both inclusive) shall not be put in force in order to acquire land for any Company, unless with the previous consent of the Local Government, and unless the Company shall have executed the agreement hereinafter mentioned.

Consent of Local Government to acquisition.

Execution of agreement.

48. Such consent shall not be given unless the Local Government be satisfied, by an enquiry held as hereinafter provided—

Previous enquiry.

(1) that such acquisition is needed for the construction of some work, and

(2) that such work is likely to prove useful to the public.

Such enquiry shall be held by such officer and at such time and place as the Local Government shall appoint.

Such officer may summon and enforce the attendance of witnesses, and compel the production of documents by the same means and, as far as possible, in the same manner as is provided by the Code of Civil Procedure in the case of a Civil Court.

49. Such officer shall report to the Local Government the result of the enquiry, and if the Local Government is satisfied that the proposed acquisition is needed for the construction of a work, and that such work is likely to prove useful to the public, it shall, subject to such rules as the Governor-General of India in Council may from time to time prescribe in this behalf, require the Company to enter into an agreement with the Secretary of State for India in Council, providing to the satisfaction of the Local Government for the following matters, namely :—

Agreement with Secretary of State in Council.

(1) The payment to Government of the cost of the acquisition :

(2) The transfer, on such payment, of the land to the Company :

(3) The terms on which the land shall be held by the Company :

(4) The time within which, and the conditions on which, the work shall be executed and maintained ; and

(5) The terms on which the public shall be entitled to use the work.

50. Every such agreement shall, as soon as may be after its execution, be published in the *Gazette of India* and also in the local official Gazette, and shall thereupon (so far as regards the terms on which the public shall be entitled to use the work) have the same effect as if it had formed part of this Act.

Publication of agreement.

This part of the Act takes the place of Act XXII of 1863, a "rather complicated measure" of fifty-three sections, "which had been hardly ever brought into practical effect." That Act "contained many conditions regarding the acquisition of land required for Railway construction by private persons or Companies other than the guaranteed Companies by which the existing Railways had been made. There had been no case," said Mr. Strachey when presenting the Report of the Select Committee, "in which these particular provisions relating to Railways had been put in force, nor was there any present probability of their being required, because no such Railways were under construction, nor were any such, he believed, contemplated."

By this part of the Act land may be compulsorily acquired by Companies for works of public utility with the previous sanction of the Local Government, subject to such rules as the Governor-General of India in Council may from time to time lay down; but such sanction is not to be given unless after enquiry the Local Government is satisfied that the acquisition is necessary for the construction of a work of public utility, and the Company execute an agreement specifying, amongst other matters (enumerated in s. 49), the terms on which the public shall be entitled to use the work.

PART VIII.

MISCELLANEOUS.

51. Service of any notice under this Act shall be made by delivering or tendering a copy thereof signed, in the case of a notice under section four, by the officer therein mentioned, and, in the case of any other notice, by or by order of the Collector or the Judge.

Service of notice.

Whenever it may be practicable, the service of the notice shall be made on the person therein named.

When such person cannot be found, the service may be made on any adult male member of his family residing with him; and if no such adult male member can be found, the notice may be served by fixing the copy on the outer door of the house in which the person therein named ordinarily dwells or carries on busines.

52. Whoever wilfully obstructs any person in doing any of the acts authorized by section four or section eight, or wilfully fills up, destroys, damages or displaces any trench or mark made under section four shall, on conviction before a Magistrate, be liable to imprisonment for any term not exceeding one month, or to fine not exceeding fifty rupees, or to both.

Obstruction to survey, &c. Filling trenches. Destroying land-marks.

53. If the Collector is opposed or impeded in taking possession under this Act of any land, he shall, if a Magistrate, enforce the surrender of the land to himself, and if not a Magistrate, he shall apply to a Magistrate or (within the Towns of Calcutta, Madras and Bombay) to the Commissioner of Police, and such Magistrate or Commissioner (as the case may be) shall enforce the surrender of the land to the Collector.

Magistrate to enforce surrender.

54. Except in the case provided for in section forty-four, nothing in this Act shall be taken to compel the Government to complete the acquisition of any land, unless an award shall have been made or a reference directed under the provisions hereinbefore contained.

Government not bound to complete acquisition.

But whenever the Government declines to complete any such acquisition, the Collector shall determine the amount of compensation due for the damage (if any)

Compensation when acquisition is not completed.

done to such land under section four or section eight and not already paid for under section five, and shall pay such amount to the person injured.

> This section was new, its object being to prevent the introduction into this country of the English rule that a notice to treat is held to be a statuteable agreement, upon which, if not duly carried out, an action for damages and a mandamus may be sustained—*Morgan* v. *Metropolitan Railway Company*, L. R., 3 C. P. 553; 4 *Ibid*, 97. But it is compulsory on Government to complete the acquisition if a reference has been directed or an award made.
>
> The Collector's decision under the second clause of this section is final. If the Government declines to complete the acquisition, a suit for compensation must be instituted within one year from the date of refusal. Act XV of 1877, sched. ii, art. 18.

55. The provisions of this Act shall not be put in force for the purpose of acquiring a part only of any house, manufactory or other building, if the owner desire that the whole of such house, manufactory or building shall be so acquired.

Part of house or building not to be taken.

> Under Act VI of 1857, s. 32, it was held that a well in a mill compound from which the mill's engine was supplied with water was part of the manufactory within the meaning of the Act—*Kharshedji Nusserwanjee* v. *The Secretary of State in Council for India*, 5 Bom. Rep., O. C. 98. In the same case, however, it was held that the owners of the mill by appointing an arbitrator before they made any claim under the section in question, had waived any irregularity in the previous proceedings and precluded themselves from claiming to have the whole manufactory taken, though no proceedings were taken in the arbitration for nearly twelve months subsequently and the defendants had shortly before such proceedings made such a claim. Similarly, under Act II of 1861, s. 5, a requisition to acquire permanently land needed for temporary occupation only, had to be made before the compensation was agreed to, or before the matter was referred to arbitration.
>
> Neither the Judge nor the High Court in appeal has power to decide any question arising under this section in the course

of a reference under this Act. "There is no express power in any section given to decide that question, and it does not arise by any reasonable inference under a reference to award compensation or a reference to apportion compensation. It is not necessary for us to say how that question can properly be raised; it may be, and very likely is, that the only way is by a suit brought for the purpose, as was certainly done in *Kharshedji Nasarvanji Cama* v. *The Secretary of State in Council* (5 Bom. Rep., O. C. 98) under the earlier Act"—*Taylor* v. *The Collector of Purneah*, I. L. R., 14 Cal. 423.

The following English decisions in this matter may be useful:—

The word 'house' comprises not only the courtyard, but also the office-houses and garden, and all that is necessary to the enjoyment of the house, if within the same ambit or circuit, whether attached to the main building or not, and though purchased subsequently to the erection of the main building—*The Governors of St. Thomas's Hospital* v. *Charing Cross Railway Co.*, 30 L. J. Ch. 395. When a railway intersected a garden and orchard attached to a mansion, the Company was held bound to take the entire property—*King* v. *Wycombe Railway Co.*, 29 L. J., Ch. 462. Houses in course of construction are houses within the meaning of the section—*Alexander* v. *West End and Crystal Palace Railway Co.*, 31 L. J., Ch. 500. The test is, would the land required pass in a conveyance of the house as a part of the appurtenances—*Fergusson* v. *London, Brighton and South Coast Railway Co.*, 2 N. R., 503, 506; *Smith* v. *Martin*, 2 Wms. Saun. 500.

But the Government is not bound to take any land which is not necessary for the convenient occupation of the house, but only subsidiary thereto—*Steele* v. *Midland Railway Co.*, L. R., 1 Ch. App. 275; *Ferguson* v. *London, Brighton and South Coast Railway Co.*, 33 L. J., Ch. 29.

Where a manufactory was partly worked by water power supplied by a reservoir, which reservoir was supplied by a goit into which water was turned from a natural stream at some distance from the manufactory, and at the point where the goit commenced, there was a weir with shuttles and a residence for a man to see to the shuttles, and a Railway Company proposed to take the weir, shuttles, residence and part of the goit, it was held that they were bound to take the whole of the manufactory—*Furniss* v. *Midland Railway Company*, L. R., 6 Eq. Ca. 473. A vacant piece of land in front of a public-house which had always passed with the lease of the house and formed the only means of approach for vehicles, was held to be part of the house—*Marson* v. *London, Chatham and Dover Ry. Co.*, L. R., 6 Eq. Ca. 101. And if the ground can fairly be considered part of the house as a residence, it is immaterial that part of it may be used for business purposes, as *e. g.* a nursery garden—*Salter* v. *Metropolitan District Railway*, L. R., 9 Eq. Ca. 432.

"The cases which have been decided upon this provision have already gone far enough. In my experience Companies have rather been the victims of the Statute than individuals. At the same time I am quite disposed to adhere to the rule which has been laid down, that it shall be construed liberally for the owner of property." *Per* the LORD CHANCELLOR, in *Reddin* v. *Metropolitan Board of Works*, 31 L. J., Ch. 660.

It has been ruled that making a tunnel under a building is taking part of the building, but that throwing an arch over it is not.

Under s. 54 the Government may withdraw, if required to take the whole building.

The state of the property at the time the notice is given is to be considered in deciding whether or not it is part of a house or building—*Sparrow* v. *Oxford &c. Railway Co.*, 2 De G. M. & G. 94.

56. Where the provisions of this Act are put in force for the purpose of acquiring land at the cost of any Municipal Fund, or of any Company, the charges incurred by the Collector in such acquisition shall be defrayed from or by such Fund or Company.

Payment of Collector's charges by Municipal Body or Company.

The charges will, of course, include any costs payable by the Collector under s. 33, as well as any expenses incurred under ss. 8, 9, 11, 17, 43, 44 or 54.

57. No award or agreement made under this Act shall be chargeable with stamp-duty, and no person claiming under any such

Exemption from stamp-duty and fees.

award or agreement shall be liable to pay any fee for a copy of the same.

> Any fee, *i.e.*, costs of any kind. Claims for compensation under the Act are also exempted from stamp-duty under Act VII of 1870, s. 19, cl. xxii.

Bar of suits to set aside awards under Act.

58. No suit shall be brought to set aside an award under this Act.

Limitation of suits for any thing done in pursuance of Act.

And no suit or other proceeding shall be commenced or prosecuted against any person for anything done in pursuance of this Act, without giving to such person a month's previous notice in writing of the intended proceeding and of the cause thereof, nor after tender of sufficient amends.

> A suit brought under the proviso to s. 40, is not a suit to set aside the award—*Kaminee Debia* v. *Protap Chunder Sandyal*, 25 W. R. 103.
>
> Under Act VI of 1857, s. 31, an award of arbitrators could be set aside by a Civil Court only on the ground of corruption or misconduct of the arbitrators.
>
> "I think the term 'award' used in s. 58 does not include the decision of the Court under s. 39. But this section indicates the intention of the Legislature to make proceedings under this Act final, and to make the mode of dealing with the questions to be raised under the Act exhaustive and self-contained." *Per* JACKSON, J. in *Nilmonee Singh Deo* v. *Rambundhoo Roy*, I. L. R., 4 Cal. 760; 3 C. L. R. 220.
>
> It has been held in England that the parties are confined to the specific remedy given by the Statute, and have no choice of any other tribunal to settle the amends in any case under the Act—*Boyfield* v. *Porter*, 13 East 208. So that persons seeking to avail themselves of the provisions of the Statute are bound to follow the particular remedy given and no other (*Mayor, &c. of Blackburn* v. *Parkinson*, 28 L. J., M. C. 7), unless the statutory remedy does not extend to and cover the whole right—*Shepherd* v. *Hills*, 11 Exch. 67.

As to the period of limitation for suits for acts done in pursuance of the Statute, see Act XV of 1877, sched. ii, art. 2. The provision in this section as to limitation was repealed by Act IX of 1871.

59. The Local Government shall have power to make rules consistent with this Act for the guidance of officers in all matters connected with its enforcement, and may from time to time alter and add to the rules so made.

Power to make rules.

All such rules, alterations and additions shall, when sanctioned by the Governor-General in Council, be published in the local official Gazette, and shall thereupon have the force of law.

Publication of rules.

This section gives to the Local Government the power of making rules consistent with the Act for the guidance of its executive officers in matters connected with its administration; and most of the Local Governments have availed themselves of this power. But the rules so made will not have the force of law or be binding upon the Courts, unless they have been sanctioned by the Governor-General in Council under this section and published in the local official Gazette. Rules having the force of law have been sanctioned for Bengal, and apparently for Bombay, though it is not quite clear that the latter were formally sanctioned as rules having the force of law under this section. The rules, however, are given below.

Rules promulgated by the Government of Bengal under section 59 of the Act.

(Published in the "Calcutta Gazette" of 7th July 1875, page 818.)

WHEREAS the basis of compensation to be awarded for revenue-paying lands taken up under the provisions of Act X of 1870 is intended by the said Act to be the actual price for which the land, subject to all its burdens, and among others to the burden of the payment of land-revenue, would sell in the market, it is necessary that the exact amount of the revenue demand should be ascertained and recorded before the award of compensation can be determined; and whereas, under the provisions of the existing law, the Revenue authorities, and none other, can regulate the amount of the revenue charge to be enforced against an estate, or a portion of an estate; and whereas some of the rules already promulgated under section 59 of the said Act proceed on assumptions which are at variance with the principle above enunciated, the following revised rules are issued by the Government of Bengal, with the sanction of the Governor-General in Council, in supersession of those previously in force:—

I.—Whenever any revenue-paying land shall be acquired under the Act, the proprietor shall, except as provided in Rule VI, be relieved of liability to pay revenue to the extent of the Government demand upon the said land; and such relief shall have effect from the date on which the Collector may take possession of the land on account of Government.

II.—In such cases the Collector shall, before making a tender or a reference to a Court regarding compensation, ascertain in accordance with the following rule, and record, the amount of Government revenue which is to be taken as payable in respect of the acquired portion; and shall, in event of a reference being made to a Court, furnish the Court, at the time of making the reference, with particulars of the amount of the share so ascertained and recorded.

III.—If the land to be acquired be an entire estate or tenure assessed with a specific amount of revenue, the whole of such amount shall be remitted.

IV.—If the land be not liable for a specific amount of revenue, but be a portion of an estate or tenure which is liable for a specific amount, the proportion of Government revenue to be deemed payable in respect of the land taken shall be ascertained under the following rules:—

1st.—When an estate has, within twenty years next preceding the date of commencement of proceedings for acquisition of any land situate therein, been subjected to a detailed settlement, or has formed portion of an estate brought under division under Regulation XIX of 1814,* made after inquiry into and record of the assets of the estate, the Government revenue to be deemed payable in respect of the said land shall bear to the assets of the said land the same proportion as the Government revenue of the whole estate bears to the assets of the whole estate, as shown in the settlement or division proceedings.

2nd.—When there may have been no such settlement or division as aforesaid, then, if the area of the estate is known with accuracy, the amount of Government revenue to be deemed payable in respect of the portion of the land taken shall bear to the Government revenue of the whole estate the same proportion as the area of the said portion bears to the area of the whole estate.

3rd.—When the Government revenue deemed payable in respect of the land taken cannot be determined by either of the above rules, one-fourth of the net rent (*i.e.*, the gross rental less a deduction of 10 per cent. for the expenses of collection) of the said land, shall be taken to be the amount of Government revenue thereon chargeable.

---

* In the territories under the Lieutenant-Governor of Bengal this Regulation has been superseded by Act VIII (B.C.) of 1876.

V.—In determining the amount of compensation to be tendered, the Collector shall take into consideration the fact that the land acquired is subject to the burden of the payment of Government revenue.

VI.—In the event of the proprietor declining to accept an abatement of revenue, such circumstance shall not entitle him to any compensation over and above the amount tendered on the original basis of calculation. In cases, however, in which the area of the portion of land acquired does not exceed more than one-twentieth part of the area of the estate, it shall be competent to the Revenue authorities, if the proprietor of the estate so desire, to pay to the proprietor the computed value of the revenue deemed payable in respect of such portion, on the condition of his continuing to pay the revenue of the entire estate without abatement : provided that, in computing the value of the revenue so assigned, the basis of calculation shall not exceed the number of years' purchase (if known) upon which the market-value of the proprietor's profits, *i.e.*, the tender of compensation, has been determined. Thus, if the market-value of the said profits has been computed at 12 years' purchase, the capitalized value of the revenue deemed payable in respect of the portion of land acquired shall be calculated at not more than 12 years' purchase of the amount of revenue in question.

VII.—When there is any doubt whether the land to be acquired is part of a revenue-paying estate or is revenue-free, the Collector shall, before making the reference to the Court, which under the circumstances he would be required to make by section 15 of the Act, determine the amount of revenue which would be deemed payable in respect of the land acquired in the event of the land being adjudged by the Court to be a portion of the revenue-paying estate of which it is alleged to form a part.

VIII.—To enable the Collector to calculate accurately the additional compensation to be given under section 42 of the Act, and to enable him to keep up fully and clearly his registers of all lands occupied and compensation paid for them, the Collector shall invariably record separately his finding under the first head of section 24 of the Act, which concerns the market-value of the land, and also the specific portion of the compensation which he may award for any houses, trees or crops upon the land.

IX.—The procedure laid down for a reference under section 15 shall be held applicable to a reference under section 43.

X.—The procedure to be followed in the apportionment of the compensation awarded on account of lands taken up for temporary occupation shall be in accordance with the provisions of Part IV of the Act.

XI.—On the date on which payment of compensation in any case may become due under section 41 of the Act, the Collector shall tender the amount to such of the persons entitled to receive it as may be present at his office, in person or by agent duly authorized to receive the same, informing them at the same time that in the event of their refusal to accept the amount tendered no claim to interest will be entertained. Should any such person be absent and have no authorized agent at the Collector's Court, the Collector shall serve a notice upon him, calling upon him to attend in person or by agent, within one week of his receipt of the notice, to receive the amount due to him, and warning him that, on failure to appear within the period above named, no interest whatever will be paid to him. Should such person neglect to appear within the time specified, the Collector shall, on being satisfied of the due service of the notice, hold the amount in deposit until it shall be applied for by the person entitled to it.

Rules promulgated by the Government of Bombay under section 59 of the Act.

(*Published in the "Bombay Gazette" of* 13*th March* 1873.)

1.—Whenever it shall appear to the Collector desirable that the Government revenue or huks of any kind shall be remitted in payment or part payment of the compensation to be awarded for land taken under this Act, he shall estimate the value of such revenue or huks, and deduct it from the estimated compensation to be awarded to the owner of the land.

2.—If the land has been surveyed and assessed to the land-revenue under the provisions of Act I of 1865, or when it bears an assessment according to existing practice, the value of the Government claims on such land shall be calculated at not less than twenty-five times the survey assessment; but houses, trees, crops, wells and improvements, shall be estimated separately on the best information available to the Collector.

3.—When the land to be taken under this Act has not been so surveyed and assessed under Act I of 1865, or does not bear an assessment according to existing practice, the Collector shall proceed to assess it on the best information he can procure, and the value of the Government claims on such lands shall be calculated at not less than twenty-five times the assessment fixed by the Collector with the approval of the Revenue Commissioner.

4.—When making an award of compensation to be given under section 42 of Act X of 1870, the Collector or Court shall record separately the compensation to be granted under the first clause of section 24 of the Act, which concerns the market-value of the land, and the portion of compensation to be granted under the 2nd, 3rd and 4th clauses of that section.

5.—The procedure required for a reference under section 15 shall be applicable to a reference under section 43.

6.—When the amount of compensation to be awarded under section 43 (for temporary occupation of land) has been fixed, and there is dispute as to the division of the amount among the persons interested, the Collector shall refer such dispute to the Court for decision, and the procedure prescribed by section 39 shall be applicable to such a reference.

7.—Any informality in the proceedings of the Collector or Court under this Act, shall not vitiate the award, unless the interest of any party or parties are injuriously affected thereby.

In no other province have any rules been promulgated having the force of law under this section. But in nearly every province and administration, instructions have been issued for the guidance of executive officers concerned in carrying out the provisions of the Act. To insert all these executive orders would not only unduly swell the bulk of this work, but would be inconsistent with its object as an exposition of the *law* on the subject of the compulsory acquisition of land in India.

THE LAND ACQUISITION (MINES) ACT, 1885.

CONTENTS.

SECTIONS.
1. Short title, commencement, and local extent.
2. Saving for mineral rights of the Government.
3. Declaration that mines are not needed.
4. Notice to be given before working mines lying under land.
5. Power to prevent or restrict working.
6. Mode of determining persons interested and amount of compensation.
7. If Local Government does not offer to pay compensation, mines may be worked in a proper manner.
8. Mining communications.
9. Local Government to pay compensation for injury done to mines.
10. And also for injury arising from any airway or other work.
11. Power to officer of Local Government to enter and inspect the working of mines.
12. Penalty for refusal to allow inspection.
13. If mines worked contrary to provisions of this Act, Local Government may require means to be adopted for safety of land acquired.
14. Construction of Act when land acquired has been transferred to a local authority or Company.
15. Pending cases.
16. Definition of local authority and Company.
17. This Act to be read with Land Acquisition Act, 1870.

ACT No. XVIII OF 1885.

PASSED BY THE GOVERNOR GENERAL OF INDIA IN COUNCIL.

(*Received the assent of the Governor General on the* 16*th October,* 1885.)

An Act to provide for cases in which Mines or Minerals are situate under land which it is desired to acquire under the Land Acquisition Act, 1870.

WHEREAS it is expedient to provide for cases in which mines or minerals are situate under land which it is desired to acquire under the Land Acquisition Act, 1870; It is hereby enacted as follows:—

1. (1) This Act may be called "The Land Acquisition (Mines) Act, 1885;" and

Short title, commencement and local extent.

(2) It shall come into force at once.

(3) It extends in the first instance to the territories administered by the Governor of Madras in Council and the Lieutenant Governor of Bengal, but any other Local Government may, from time to time, by notification in the official Gazette, extend this Act to the whole or any specified part of the territories under its administration.

The following is taken from the Statement of Objects and Reasons published at the time the Act was introduced into the Legislative Council:—

The object of this Bill is to provide for cases in which mines or minerals are situate under land which it is desired to acquire under the Land Acquisition Act, 1870.

Act XXII of 1863, which was replaced by the Land Acquisition Act, 1870, contained specific provisions (ss. 51 and 52) for cases in which mines and minerals lay under land taken up under that Act. These provisions were not, however, re-enacted in the Act of 1870, which, as the Government is advised, contemplates the acquisition of the underlying minerals as well as the surface of the land.

Hitherto this state of the law has caused no inconvenience. Now, however, owing to its being proposed to extend railways across districts where there is a certain amount of coal to be found, notice has been drawn to the inconvenience of the existing law, which practically compels the Government either to purchase all the mines and minerals under the land over which it is proposed to construct a line or to abandon the undertaking altogether.

Under these circumstances, the present Bill has been prepared. It does not, however, simply re-enact the provisions which Act XXII of 1863 formerly contained, inasmuch as they do not appear to be adapted to the circumstances of the case. It follows rather the rules contained in the English Railway Clauses Consolidation Act, 1845 (8 Vict., c. 20, s. 77 *et seq.*), which it extends to the acquisition of land for all purposes and not merely for the construction of railways.

Saving for mineral rights of the Government.

2. Except as expressly provided by this Act, nothing in this Act shall affect the right of the Government to any mines or minerals.

The right of Government to mines and minerals has been expressly declared in certain local statutes. Thus, the Punjab Land Revenue Act XXXIII of 1871, s. 29 :—" Mines of metal or coal and goldwashings shall in every case be deemed to be the property of Government; but if Government works or causes to be worked any such mine, compensation for damage to the surface of the soil shall be made to the owner of such surface. Such compensation may be claimed and shall be ascertained and awarded in accordance with the provisions of Act X of 1870." Similarly, s. 3 of the Ajmir Land and Revenue Regulation II of 1877 provides that " except in the case of lands in respect of which istimrári sanads have been granted by the Chief Commissioner with the previous sanction of the Governor General in Council, the Government shall be presumed until the contrary is proved to be the sole owner of all mines, opened and unopened, of metal, coal and other valuable minerals, with full liberty to search for and work the same."

And s. 151 of the *Central Provinces Land Revenue Act*, XVIII of

1881, provides that, unless it is otherwise expressly provided in the records of a settlement or by the terms of a grant made by Government, the right to all mines, minerals, coal and quarries shall be deemed to belong to Government; and the Government shall have all powers necessary for the proper enjoyment of such rights: Provided that whenever in the exercise by the Government of the rights herein referred to over any land, the rights of any persons are infringed by the occupation or disturbance of the surface of such land, the Government shall pay to such persons compensation for such infringement, and the amount of such compensation shall be determined as nearly as may be in accordance with the provisions of the Land Acquisition Act, 1870.

3. (1) When the Local Government makes a declaration under section 6 of the Land Acquisition Act, 1870, that land is needed for a public purpose or for a Company, it may, if it thinks fit, insert in the declaration a statement that the mines of coal, iron-stone, slate or other minerals lying under the land or any particular portion of the land, except only such parts of the mines or minerals as it may be necessary to dig or carry away or use in the construction of the work for the purpose of which the land is being acquired, are not needed.

Declaration that mines are not needed.

(2) When a statement as aforesaid has not been inserted in the declaration made in respect of any land under section 6 of the Land Acquisition Act, 1870, and the Collector is of opinion that the provisions of this Act ought to be applied to the land, he may abstain from tendering compensation under section 11 of the said Land Acquisition Act in respect of the mines, and may—

(a) when he makes an award under section 14 of that Act, insert such a statement in his award;

(b) when he makes a reference to the Court under section 15 of that Act, insert such a statement in his reference; or

(c) when he takes possession of the land under section 17 of that Act, publish such a statement in such manner as the Governor General in Council may, from time to time, prescribe.

(3) If any such statement is inserted in the declaration, award or reference, or published as aforesaid, the mines of coal, iron-stone, slate or other minerals under the land or portion of the land specified in the statement, except as aforesaid, shall not vest in the Government when the land so vests under the said Act.

> A mine has been defined to be a way or passage underground; and a quarry to be a stone-pit, a place upon or above, and not under the ground. In *Bell* v. *Wilson* (34 L. J., Ch. 572; 35 L. J., Ch. 337; L. R., 1 Ch. Ap. 303), it was held that the reservation in a conveyance of "mines, metals or minerals" included freestone; but that under the reservation the stone could not be worked except by means of underground workings. The term minerals, properly speaking, includes only such substances as are dug out of the earth by means of a pit or covered tunnel and does not include, for instance, limestone rock which is worked by means of a quarry. (*Darvill* v. *Roper*, 24 L. J., Ch. 779.) But there appears to be no fixed principle upon which the Courts will interpret the word. They will in general interpret it according to the nature of the instrument in which it occurs and the circumstances under which the instrument is framed—*Bell* v. *Wilson* (*supra*).

4. If the person for the time being immediately entitled to work or get any mines or minerals lying under any land so acquired is desirous of working or getting the same, he shall give the Local Government notice in writing of his intention so to do sixty days before the commencement of working.

Notice to be given before working mines lying under land.

> The length of notice prescribed by the English statute is thirty days only—8 & 9 Vict., c. 20, s. 78.

5. (1) At any time or times after the receipt of a notice

Power to prevent or restrict working. under the last foregoing section, and whether before or after the expiration of the said period of sixty days, the Local Government may cause the mines or minerals to be inspected by a person appointed by it for the purpose ; and

(2) If it appears to the Local Government that the working or getting of the mines or minerals, or any part thereof, is likely to cause damage to the surface of the land or any work thereon, the Local Government may publish, in such manner as the Governor General in Council may, from time to time, direct, a declaration of its willingness, either—

(*a*) to pay compensation for the mines or minerals still unworked or ungotten, or that part thereof, to all persons having an interest in the same ; or

(*b*) to pay compensation to all such persons in consideration of those mines or minerals, or that part thereof, being worked or gotten in such manner and subject to such restrictions as the Local Government may in its declaration specify.

(3) If the declaration mentioned in case (*a*) is made, then those mines or minerals, or that part thereof, shall not thereafter be worked or gotten by any person.

(4) If the declaration mentioned in case (*b*) is made, then those mines or minerals, or that part thereof, shall not thereafter be worked or gotten by any person save in the manner and subject to the restrictions specified by the Local Government.

> The principle of the present Act is that compensation need not be paid for minerals at the time the land is acquired, but if subsequently the owner desires to work them, the Government must pay compensation if it is necessary to prevent him from working them in the most beneficial manner.

6. When the working or getting of any mines or minerals has been prevented or restricted under section 5, the persons interested in those mines or minerals and the amounts of compensation payable to them respectively shall, subject to all necessary modifications, be ascertained in the manner provided by the Land Acquisition Act, 1870, for ascertaining the persons interested in the land to be acquired under that Act and the amounts of compensation payable to them, respectively.

Mode of determining persons interested and amount of compensation.

> The lessee of mines, whose term is of sufficient length to enable him by working with reasonable diligence to exhaust them, is, for the purpose of this section, the absolute owner thereof; and the Company having paid him compensation are in the position of absolute owner of the minerals in perpetuity; and neither the reversioner nor any person claiming under him is entitled to any compensation other than for the loss of royalty by reason of the non-working of the mines—*Great Western Rail. Co.* v. *Smith,* 45 L. J., Ch. 235.
>
> In *Barnsley Canal Co.* v. *Twill,* 13 L. J., Ch. 234, the Company had purchased of the lessor all his interest in the coals which they had required him to abstain from working. It was held that they were also bound to compensate the lessee for the loss of profits on such coals. A coal owner is also entitled to compensation for any injury he may sustain by having to work the mine in a less beneficial manner for the sake of not injuring the Company—*Cromford Canal Co.* v. *Cutts and another,* 5 Rail. Ca., 442.

7. (1) If before the expiration of the said sixty days, the Local Government does not publish a declaration as provided in section 5, the owner, lessee, or occupier of the mines may, unless and until such a declaration is subsequently made, work the mines or any part thereof in a manner proper and necessary for

If Local Government does not offer to pay compensation, mines may be worked in a proper manner.

the beneficial working thereof, and according to the usual manner of working such mines in the local area where the same are situate.

(2) If any damage or obstruction is caused to the surface of the land or any works thereon by improper working of the mines, the owner, lessee or occupier of the mines shall at once, at his own expense, repair the damage or remove the obstruction, as the case may require.

(3) If the repair or removal is not at once effected, or, if the Local Government so thinks fit, without waiting for the same to be effected by the owner, lessee or occupier, the Local Government may execute the same and recover from the owner, lessee or occupier the expense occasioned thereby.

> "The Company can stop all dangerous working at any time they think fit, and they are the sole judges of when the working becomes dangerous, provided they act within reasonable limits." *Per* LORD ROMILLY in *Midland Rail. Co.* v. *Checkley,* 36 L. J., Ch. 380.
>
> In *The Caledonian Rail. Co.* v. *Sprot* (2 Macq. Sc. Ap. 449) it was held that a person selling land for a railway impliedly sells all necessary support, both subjacent and adjacent, that is required for the purpose of supporting that railway. That decision, however, was given before the passing of the Railway Clauses Consolidation Act and was a decision upon a contract. The case of *Elliott* v. *The North-Eastern Rail. Co.* (10 H. L. C. 333 ; 32 L. J., Ch. 402) also turned upon a private Act of Parliament, in which it was held that there was " nothing to exclude the ordinary right of a purchaser to such support of the land which he has bought, both subjacent and adjacent, as the common law of the land gives him. " The leading case under the Railway Clauses Consolidation Act is that of *The Great Western Rail. Co.* v. *Bennett* (L. R., 2 H. L. 27), in which Lord CRANWORTH said:—"It was obviously the intention of the Legislature in making these provisions to create a new Code as to the relation between mine owners and Railway Companies where lands were compulsorily taken for the purposes of a railway. The object of the statute evidently was to get rid of all the ordinary law on the subject, and to compel the owner to sell the surface, and

if any mines were so near the surface that they must be taken for the purposes of the railway, to compel him to sell them, but not to compel him to sell anything more. The land was to be dealt with just as if there were no mines to be considered— nothing but the surface. That being so, justice obviously requires that when the mine owner thinks it beneficial to him to work his mines, and proceeds to do so, he should be just in the same position as if he had never sold any part of the surface at all. If he had not compulsorily parted with the surface, he might have worked his mines, sinking his shaft from the very surface down to the very bottom of the mine. The object of the statute was that, for the purpose of the railway, the Company was to take (and it was a very beneficial provision for the Company) that and that only which is necessary for the purpose of the railway, and that all the rest should be left to be dealt with, whenever the time for working the mine should arrive." Similarly Lord WESTBURY said:—"In the face of these words (of the statute) there is no room for the ordinary implication which applies to a common grant, namely, that it extends by implication to all that, though not named, which is necessary for the support or enjoyment of the thing granted. Then what relation remains between the Railway Company and the mine owner? It is defined by the statute. Although the mines *in solido* are, without any exception, reserved to the mine owner, he is not at liberty to win them or to proceed to get them without notice to the Railway Company. That notice expires after a month. During that month the Railway Company is under an obligation to ascertain whether it may be requisite for the support of the railway to purchase any part of the subjacent minerals. If the Company should not think it requisite, the mine owner is left under no other obligation than that he is to win the mines in a proper manner; and if there is a custom of the country, it must be done according to that custom; and the Railway Company is armed with authority to inspect the working from time to time in order to ascertain whether any damage is likely to ensue, or whether any proceeding of the mine owner is inconsistent with the ordinary beneficial manner of winning the minerals. The relation, therefore, between the Railway Company and the mine owner is one so clearly defined, so useful to the Railway Company and at the same time so fair and just to the mine owner, that one is astonished that any argument could have been raised upon the ordinary implication applicable to a grant, which is so entirely excluded by the express enactment of the statute, and also by the accompanying provisions that define, beyond the possibility of mistake, the true relation, which, after the land has been conveyed to the Railway Company, continues to exist between the Company and the mine owner."

8. If the working of any mines is prevented or restricted under section 5, the respective owners, lessees and occupiers of the mines, if their mines extend so as to lie on both sides of the mines, the working of which is prevented or restricted, may cut and make such and so many airways, headways, gateways or water-levels through the mines, measures or strata, the working whereof is prevented or restricted, as may be requisite to enable them to ventilate, drain and work their said mines; but no such airway, headway, gateway or water-level shall be of greater dimensions or section than may be prescribed by the Governor General in Council in this behalf, and, where no dimensions are so prescribed not greater than eight feet wide and eight feet high, nor shall the same be cut or made upon any part of the surface or works, or so as to injure the same, or to interfere with the use thereof.

Mining communications.

9. The Local Government shall, from time to time, pay to the owner, lessee or occupier of any such mines extending so as to lie on both sides of the mines, the working of which is prevented or restricted, all such additional expenses and losses as may be incurred by him by reason of the severance of the lands lying over those mines or of the continuous working of those mines being interrupted as aforesaid, or by reason of the same being worked in such manner and under such restrictions as not to prejudice or injure the surface or works, and for any minerals not acquired by the Local Government which cannot

Local Government to pay compensation for injury done to mines.

be obtained by reason of the action taken under the foregoing sections; and if any dispute or question arises between the Local Government and the owner, lessee or occupier as aforesaid, touching the amount of those losses or expenses, the same shall be settled as nearly as may be in the manner provided for the settlement of questions touching the amount of compensation payable under the Land Acquisition Act, 1870.

> This section is supplementary to s. 6.

10. If any loss or damage is sustained by the owner or occupier of the lands lying over any such mines, the working whereof has been so prevented or restricted as aforesaid, and not being the owner, lessee or occupier of those mines, by reason of the making of any such airway or other works as aforesaid, which or any like work it would not have been necessary to make but for the working of the mines having been so prevented or restricted as aforesaid, the Local Government shall pay full compensation to that owner or occupier of the surface lands for the loss or damage so sustained by him.

And also for injury arising from any airway or other work.

> This section provides for compensation for damage sustained by the owner of adjacent lands, who is not also the owner of the mines.

11. For better ascertaining whether any mines lying under land acquired in accordance with the provisions of this Act are being worked, or have been worked, or are likely to be worked, so as to damage the land or the works thereon, an officer appointed for this purpose by the Local Government may, after giving twenty-four hours' notice in writing, enter into and return from any such mines or the works connected therewith; and for that purpose the officer so appointed may make use of any apparatus or machinery belonging

Power to officer of Local Government to enter and inspect the working of mines.

to the owner, lessee or occupier of the mines, and use all necessary means for discovering the distance from any part of the land acquired to the parts of the mines which have been, are being, or are about to be worked.

12. If any owner, lessee or occupier of any such mines

Penalty for refusal to allow inspection.

or works refuses to allow any officer appointed by the Local Government for that purpose to enter into and inspect any such mines or works in manner aforesaid, he shall be punished with fine which may extend to two hundred rupees.

13. If it appears that any such mines have been worked contrary to the provisions of this Act,

If mines worked contrary to provisions of this Act, Local Government may require means to be adopted for safety of land acquired.

the Local Government may, if it thinks fit, give notice to the owner, lessee or occupier thereof to construct such works and to adopt such means as may be necessary or proper for making safe the land acquired and the works thereon, and preventing injury thereto; and if, after such notice, any such owner, lessee or occupier does not forthwith proceed to construct the works necessary for making safe the land acquired and the works thereon, the Local Government may itself construct the works and recover the expense thereof from the owner, lessee or occupier.

14. When a statement under section 3 has been made

Construction of Act when land acquired has been transferred to a local authority or Company.

regarding any land, and the land has been acquired by the Government, and has been transferred to or has vested by operation of law in a local authority or Company, then sections 4 to 13, both inclusive, shall be read as if for the words "the Local Government," wherever they occur in those sections, the words "the local authority or Company, as the case may be, which has acquired the land" were substituted.

15. (1) This Act shall apply to any land for the acquisition whereof proceedings under the Land Acquisition Act, 1870, are pending at the time when this Act comes into force, unless before that time the Collector has made, in respect of the land, an award under section 14 or a reference to the Court under section 15 of that Act, or has taken possession of the land under section 17 of the same.

Pending cases.

(2) When the Collector has before the said time made an award or reference in respect of any such land or taken possession thereof as aforesaid, and all the persons interested in the land, or entitled under the Land Acquisition Act, 1870, to act for persons so interested, who have attended or may attend in the course of the proceedings under sections 11 to 15, both inclusive, of the Land Acquisition Act, 1870, consent in writing to the application of this Act to the land, the Collector may, by an order in writing, direct that it shall apply, and thereupon it shall be deemed to have applied from the commencement of the proceedings; and the Collector shall be deemed, as the case may be, to have inserted in his award or reference, or to have published in the prescribed manner, when he took possession, the statement mentioned in section 3 of this Act.

16. In this Act—

(*a*) "local authority" means any municipal committee, district board, body of port commissioners or other authority legally entitled to, or entrusted by the Government with, the control or management of any municipal or local fund; and

Definition of local authority and Company.

(*b*) "Company" means a Company registered under any of the enactments relating to Companies from time to time in force in British India, or formed in pursuance of an Act of Parliament or by Royal Charter or Letters Patent.

It is to be observed that ss. 6 and 56 of Act X of 1870 speak of a municipal fund only, and not of a local fund. The term "local authority" does not occur in that Act.

This Act is to be read with and taken as part of Act X of 1870. But "Company" is defined by s. 3 of that Act. There are therefore two definitions of the word as the law stands. This being the more general, it was probably intended to repeal the former definition: but, if so, the intention appears to have been overlooked.

17. This Act shall, for the purposes of all enactments for the time being in force, be read with and taken as part of the Land Acquisition Act, 1870.

This Act to be read with Land Acquisition Act, 1870.

APPENDIX.

The provisions of Act X of 1870 have been wholly or partially made applicable under various local Acts, which treat of the acquisition of land or the award of compensation in cognate matters. A treatise on the law of compensation would be incomplete without a reference to such Acts. It is proposed, therefore, to consider briefly the Acts of the various local Legislatures, and those Acts of the Legislative Council of India which apply to limited local areas, by which the provisions of Act X of 1870 are made applicable for any purpose whatever.

Madras.—The *Madras Salt Excise Act*, VI of 1871, contains certain provisions for awarding compensation in cases where it is considered desirable to suppress the manufacture of salt. By s. 26 notice must be given and claims to compensation invited. By s. 27 the manufacture shall cease in any work or pan from and after the date specified in the notice, *but the ownership of the land shall not be affected thereby*. By s. 29 the Collector is required to "enquire into the market-value of the saltwork or pan, if sold free of all encumbrances, deducting the value, if any, of the land and of any buildings thereon which are capable of being applied to any other purpose than the manufacture of salt." If the Collector and the registered proprietor agree as to the amount of compensation, the Collector will make an award; otherwise he is to refer the matter to the Civil Court of the district; and in ascertaining the amount of compensation, the Court is simply to take into account the matter mentioned in s. 29. A salt-work is defined by Madras Act I of 1882, s. 2, and for the purposes of this Act the registered proprietor is to be taken as the full owner thereof, and to be entitled to receive the compensation from the Collector. Certain other minor provisions are borrowed from the Land Acquisition Act.

By the *Madras Forest Act*, V of 1882, s. 68, "whenever it appears to the Governor in Council that any land is required for the purposes of the Act, such land shall be deemed to be needed for a public purpose within the meaning of the Land Acquisition Act, 1870, s. 4." And by s. 10, where a claim to a right in or over any land proposed to be included in a reserved forest is admitted wholly or in part, the Forest Settlement-Officer may proceed to acquire such land in the manner provided by the Land Acquisition Act. For the purpose of so acquiring such land—(i) the Forest Settlement-Officer shall be deemed to be a Collector proceeding under the Land Acquisition Act, 1870; (ii) the claimant shall be deemed to be a person interested and appearing before him in pursuance of a notice given under s. 9 of that Act; (iii) the provisions of the preceding sections of that Act shall be deemed to have been complied with; and (iv) the Forest Settlement-Officer, with the consent of the claimant, or the Court as defined in the said Act, with the consent of the claimant and of the Collector of the District, may award compensation by the grant of rights in or over land, or by the payment of money, or both. The same course will be followed where claims are in the first instance rejected by the Forest Settlement-Officer, but admitted on appeal to the District Court. In any such case the forest cannot be notified as a reserved forest until such land has become vested in Government under s. 16 of the Act.

By s. 29 the Governor in Council is authorized to regulate or prohibit certain acts in any forest or waste land not at the disposal of Government, and by s. 30, if the owner of such forest or land declines to comply with the regulations or directions laid down, the Government may assume control of it, and in that case the owner is bound either to lease it to Government, or to require that it be taken under the Act. If a lease is agreed upon, the amount of annual rent to be reserved and all other questions arising between the owner or persons claiming to be owners and the Government, shall, in case of dispute, be determined in accordance, so far as may be, with the provisions of the Land Acquisition Act, 1870. And by s. 31, the Government may, instead of assuming control over the forest or land, acquire it under the Act.

By the *City of Madras Municipal Act*, I of 1884, s. 443, when there is any hindrance to the acquisition by purchase of any land or building required for the purposes of the Act, the Governor in Council, upon the representation of the Commissioners, may declare that the land or building is needed for a public purpose and may order proceedings for obtaining possession of the same for the Governor in Council, and for determining the compensation to be paid to the parties interested, according to the law for the time being in force for the acquisition of land for public purposes. And the Governor in Council may vest such land or building in the Commissioners on their paying the compensation awarded. And by s. 444 the Commissioners may, with the sanction of the Governor in Council, sell any lands or buildings so acquired by them.

Land may also be acquired for a Municipal Council under the *Madras District Municipalities Act*, IV of 1884, s. 279, and for a Local Board under the *Madras Local Boards Act*, V of 1884, s. 153, and on payment of the compensation, the land vests in the Council or Board, as the case may be.

By the *Madras Rivers Conservancy Act*, VI of 1884, s. 4, all persons authorized to make a survey under the Act are vested with the powers given in ss. 4 and 5 of the Land Acquisition Act, subject to the provisoes therein contained. And ss. 16 and 17 provide for the award of compensation for certain acts done by the Conservator of Rivers, though the Act is silent as to the manner in which the compensation is to be assessed.

By the *Madras Harbour Trust Act*, II of 1886, s. 27, when the Board are unable to acquire by private contract any immoveable property required for the purposes of the Act, the Governor in Council may in his discretion declare that such property is required for a public purpose, and may order proceedings to be taken for obtaining possession of the same according to the law for the time being in force for the acquisition of land for public purposes. And such property, when so acquired, shall, on their paying the compensation awarded and all costs connected with its acquirement, be deemed to be vested in the Board.

By the *Madras Railway Protection Act*, IV of 1886, s. 16, a landholder or other person who has sustained loss or damage by any of the measures taken under the Act, is declared to be entitled to compensation, to be fixed by the Collector after such enquiry as he may deem fit. This enquiry may, on the application of the claimant, be conducted by five assessors, of whom not less than half shall be nominated by the Collector and the remainder by the claimant. If the Collector and the claimant cannot agree as to the amount of compensation, the claimant may file a suit in the Civil Court to have it determined.

BOMBAY.—Section 152 of the Bombay Act III of 1872 (Municipality of Bombay) provides penalties for the fouling of water by offensive trades, and empowers the Commissioner to lay open and examine pipes, conduits and works; and the last clause runs as follows :—" In all cases when land belonging to third parties is required for the purpose of carrying out the provisions of this section, such purpose shall be and be deemed to be a public purpose within the meaning of Act X of 1870." By s. 154 the Municipal Commissioner is authorized to lay out and improve the streets and roads, making due compensation from the Municipal Fund to the owners or occupiers of any land, house or building that may be required for the purpose. By s. 155 the Corporation may sell streets which have been closed. Section 156 empowers the Commissioner to agree with the owners for the absolute purchase of land for any purpose whatever connected with the conservancy or general improvement of the city. And s. 157 gives the Corporation power to acquire also "the land necessary for the houses and buildings to form the street," and also to dispose of the same; provided that compensation be made for any damage done to any adjoining land or buildings.

Section 289 runs thus :—" Except as herein otherwise provided, in all cases where compensation, damages, costs or expenses are by this Act directed to be paid, the amount, and, if necessary, the apportionment of the same in case of dispute, shall be ascertained and determined by the Chief Presidency Magistrate." Sections 290—292 prescribe the procedure to be followed in such cases. Then s. 293 provides that when there is any hindrance to the permanent or temporary acquisition of any land or building required for the purpose of the Act, the Government may declare that it is needed for a public purpose, and acquire it for the Corporation on their paying the compensation awarded.

Similarly s. 25 of the *Bombay District Municipal Act*, VI of 1873, provides as follows :—" When there is any hindrance to the permanent or temporary acquisition upon payment of any land or building required for the purposes of this Act, the Governor in Council may, after obtaining possession of the same under

Act X of 1870 or other existing law, vest such land or building in the municipality on their paying the compensation awarded."

By s. 34 of the *Bombay Salt Act*, VII of 1873, the Governor in Council may direct the acquisition under the Land Acquisition Act of any salt work within the Presidency with a view to its summary suppression.

Section 64 of the *Bombay Abkari Act*, V of 1878, extends the provisions of the Land Acquisition Act to the determination of the compensation to be awarded for certain exceptional rights and immunities in respect of the abkari revenue of the Poway estate in the Island of Salsette, "as if the said rights and immunities were land required for public purposes."

By s. 27 of the *Bombay Port Trust Act*, VI of 1879, " when the Board are unable to acquire by agreement any immoveable property required for the purposes of the Act, Government may in their discretion order proceedings to be taken for acquiring the same on behalf of the Board as if such property were land needed for a public purpose within the meaning of the Land Acquisition Act, 1870. The amount of compensation awarded and all other charges incurred in the acquisition of any such property shall be forthwith defrayed by the Board, and thereupon the said property shall vest in the Board."

By s. 32 Government is empowered to acquire upon payment of compensation land which has vested in the Board.

It remains to consider certain provisions of the *Bombay Irrigation Act*, VII of 1879.

Section 7 of that Act provides that "whenever it shall be necessary to make any enquiry or examination in connection with a projected canal or with the maintenance of an existing canal, any Canal-officer duly empowered in this behalf, and any person acting under the general or special order of any such Canal-officer, may exercise all powers and do all things in respect of such land as he might exercise and do, if the Government had issued a notification under the provisions of s. 4 of the Land Acquisition Act, 1870, to the effect that land in that locality is likely to be needed for a public purpose."

Under Part III of the Act when persons are unable to construct new water-courses under private arrangement with the owners of the land, they may apply to the Canal-officer to construct the water-course on their behalf. If the canal-officer consider the construction of the proposed water-course expedient, he is to mark out the land which, in his opinion, it will be necessary to occupy for the construction thereof, and publish a notification to that effect. Thereupon (s. 19) the Collector shall proceed to acquire such land under the provisions of the Land Acquisition Act, 1870, as if a declaration had been issued by the Government for the acquisition thereof under s. 6 of that Act, and as if the Government had thereupon directed the Collector to take order for the acquisition of such land under s. 7 of the said Act, and, if necessary, as if the Government had issued orders for summary possession being taken under s. 17 of the said Act.

Part V of the Act treats of the award of compensation; and the following rules are laid down :—

Section 31 says :—" Compensation may be awarded in respect of any substantial damage caused by the exercise of any of the powers conferred by this Act, which is capable of being ascertained and estimated at the time of awarding such compensation: Provided that no compensation shall be so awarded in respect of any damage arising from—

(*a*) deterioration of climate, or

(*b*) stoppage of navigation or the means of rafting timber or of watering cattle, or

(*c*) stoppage or diminution of any supply of water in consequence of the exercise of the power conferred by s. 5, if no use have been made of such supply within the five years next before the date of the issue of the notification under s. 73, or

(*d*) failure or stoppage of the water in a canal, when such failure or stoppage is due to—

(1) any cause beyond the control of Government,

(2) the execution of any repairs, alterations or additions to the canal, or

(3) any measures considered necessary by any Canal-officer duly empowered in this behalf for regulating the proper flow of water in the canal, or for maintaining the established course of irrigation;

but any person who suffers loss from any stoppage or diminution of his water-supply, due to any of the causes named in clause (*d*) of this section, shall be entitled to such remission of the water-rate payable by him as may be authorized by the Governor in Council."

Section 32.—"No claim for compensation under this Act shall be entertained after the expiration of twelve months from the time when the damage complained of commenced, unless the Collector is satisfied that the claimant had sufficient cause for not making the claim within such period."

Section 33.—"No compensation shall be claimable under this Act in respect of any work executed before it came into force, or of any damage caused by or in the execution of any such work."

Sections 34—36 treat of the summary award of compensation in certain cases by the Collector, whose decision is to be conclusive. Section 37 provides for the issue of notice by the Collector. Then s. 38 says:—"All claims for compensation under this Act other than claims of the nature provided for in ss. 34 and 35, must be made before the Collector of the District in which such claim arises." Section 39.—"The Collector shall enquire into such claim, and determine the amount of compensation, if any, which should, in his opinion, be given to the claimant; and ss. 11, 12, 14, 15, 18 to 23 (inclusive), 26 to 40 (inclusive), 51 and 58 of the Land Acquisition Act, 1870, shall apply to such enquiries: Provided that, instead of the last clause of the said s. 26, the following shall be read:—'The provisions of this section and of ss. 31 and 40 of the Bombay Irrigation Act, 1879, shall be read to every assessor in a language which he understands before he gives his opinion as to the amount of compensation to be awarded.'"

Section 40.—"In determining the amount of compensation under the last preceding section, regard shall be had to the diminution in the market-value, at the time of awarding compensation of the property in respect of which compensation is claimed; and when such market-value is not ascertainable, the amount shall be reckoned at twelve times the amount of the diminution of the annual nett profits of such property, caused by the exercise of the powers conferred by this Act."

Section 41.—"All sums of money payable for compensation

awarded under s. 39 shall become due three months after the claim for such compensation was made ; and simple interest at the rate of six per centum per annum shall be allowed on any such sum remaining unpaid after the said three months, except when the non-payment of such sum is caused by the neglect or refusal of the claimant to apply for or receive the same."

Sections 42 and 43 contain provisions for an abatement of land-revenue or rent in certain cases in which compensation has been awarded.

NORTHERN INDIA.—Act VIII of 1873 of the Supreme Legislative Council (*The Northern India Canal and Drainage Act,* 1873) formed the model of the various local Irrigation Acts, though its provisions in the matter now under consideration are not so complete as those contained in Bengal Act III of 1876. It extends to the North-Western Provinces, the Punjab, Oudh and the Central Provinces. It provides that when the water of any natural stream or lake is required for the purpose of any existing or projected canal or drainage-work, claims for compensation shall be enquired into and determined under the provisions of the Land Acquisition Act. By s. 10 the provisions of ss. 9 to 12 (inclusive), 14 & 15, 18 to 23 (inclusive), 26 to 40 (inclusive), 51, 57, 58 and 59 of the Land Acquisition Act are made applicable to the enquiry. Section 8 of Act VIII of 1873 corresponds with s. 11 of the Bengal Act, with this difference that s. 8 further provides that no compensation shall be awarded for any damage caused by *displacement of labour.*

By s. 15 of the Act any Divisional Canal-officer or any person acting under his orders in this behalf may enter upon any adjacent lands and execute all works that may be necessary for the purpose of repairing or preventing accidents to a canal ; and if such person's tender of compensation for any damage done be not accepted, the Canal-officer shall refer the matter to the Collector, who is to proceed to award compensation for the damage, as though the Local Government had directed the occupation of the lands under s. 43 of the Land Acquisition Act, 1870.

By s. 21 any person desiring the construction of a new water-course may apply to the Divisional Canal-officer, stating

that he has unsuccessfully endeavoured to acquire a right to occupy the land which will be needed for such water-course. And by s. 23 any person desiring that an existing water-course should be transferred from its present owner to himself, may similarly apply, stating that he has endeavoured unsuccessfully to procure such transfer. In these cases if the construction or transfer of the water-course is approved, the applicant may be placed in occupation. But s. 28 says :—
" No such applicant shall be placed in occupation of such land or water-course until he has paid to the person named by the Collector such an amount as the Collector determines to be due as compensation for the land or water-course so occupied or transferred, and for any damage caused by the marking out or occupation of such land, together with all expenses incidental to such occupation or transfer." In determining the compensation to be made under this section, the Collector shall proceed under the provisions of the Land Acquisition Act, 1870; but he may, if the person to be compensated so desire, award such compensation in the form of a rent-charge payable in respect of the land or water-course occupied or transferred. By s. 61, whenever an obstruction is removed or modified, or a drainage work carried out under the provisions of the Act, all claims for compensation on account of any consequential damage are to be dealt with in the manner provided in s. 10.

By s. 39 of the *North-Western and Oudh Municipalities Act* (XV of 1873 of the Supreme Legislative Council), " whenever any land within the limits of any municipality to which this Act is extended is required for the construction or improvement of a highway, for the promotion of the healthiness of the neighbourhood, or for any other public purpose, if the Committee cannot agree with the owner for the purchase thereof, the Local Government, on the recommendation of the Committee, may notify in the local official Gazette that such land is required under the provisions of the Land Acquisition Act, 1870 ; and on payment by the Committee of the compensation awarded under such Act, the land shall vest in them for the purposes of this Act."

A similar provision is contained in the *North-Western Provinces* and *Oudh Local Boards Act*, XIV of 1883, s. 50; and also in the *North-Western Provinces and Oudh Municipalities Act*, XV of 1883, s. 67.

By s. 25 of the *Punjab Land Revenue Act* (XXXIII of 1871 of the Supreme Legislative Council) settlement-officers and the servants and workmen employed by them are vested with the powers specified in s. 4 of the Land Acquisition Act for the purpose of making plans and surveys, and of collecting such information as to the quality and produce of the land as may be necessary to enable them to assess the revenue to be paid thereon.

Section 29 of the same Act provides that when Government works any mine of metal or coal, compensation for damage to the surface of the soil shall be made to the owner of the surface; and such compensation is to be claimed, ascertained and awarded in accordance with the provisions of Act X of 1870.

Similarly s. 151 of the *Central Provinces Land Revenue Act*, XVIII of 1881, provides:—"Unless it is otherwise expressly provided in the records of a settlement or by the terms of a grant made by Government, the right to all mines, minerals, coals and quarries, and to all fisheries in navigable rivers, and the right to extract sap from all palmyra and cocoa-nut trees shall be deemed to belong to Government; and the Government shall have all powers necessary for the proper enjoyment of such rights: Provided that whenever in the exercise by the Government of the rights herein referred to over any land, the rights of any persons are infringed by the occupation or disturbance of the surface of such land, the Government shall pay to such persons compensation for such infringement, and the amount of such compensation shall be determined as nearly as may be in accordance with the provisions of the Land Acquisition Act, 1870."

By s. 38 of the *Punjab Municipalities Act* (XIII of 1884 of the Supreme Legislative Council) when any land, whether within or without the limits of a municipality, is required for the purposes of the Act, the Local Government may, at the request of the Committee, acquire it under the provisions of the Land Acquisition Act, and on payment by the Committee of the compensation and other charges, the land will vest in the Committee. The provisions of the Land Acquisition Act are also by s. 125 made applicable to the determination of claims to compensation for injury to any building or land caused by the Committee or its officers and servants in the exercise of any of the powers vested in them.

AJMIR.—By the *Ajmir Land and Revenue Regulation*, II of 1877, certain modifications are introduced as regards the procedure under the Act in respect of lands acquired in an istimrári estate as defined in s. 23 of the Regulation. Section 26 runs as follows:—" When land situate in an istimrári estate is to be acquired under the Land Acquisition Act, 1870, for the purpose of constructing a railway, or for any other object which, in the opinion of the Chief Commissioner, may reasonably be expected to improve the value of such estate,

1*st*,—the determination of the Collector under s. 11 of that Act as to the amount of compensation to be allowed for such land, shall be final and conclusive;

2*nd*,—in arriving at such determination, the Collector, instead of taking into consideration the market-value of such land as required by ss. 13 and 24 of that Act, shall fix the value of such land in manner following, that is to say—

(*a*) when such land is cultivated, he shall ascertain the amount of revenue which would be assessed on such land if it were being fully assessed to land-revenue under the law for the time being in force, and shall allow twenty times the amount so ascertained; and when such land is uncultivated he shall, notwithstanding the existence of any custom by which such land would be given free of charge, ascertain the amount of revenue which would be assessed on such land if it were cultivated and were being fully assessed as aforesaid, and shall allow three times the amount so ascertained:

(*b*) he shall allow, besides the amount allowed under cl. (*a*), such further amount in respect of any trees and of any wells, tanks, embankments, houses and other works and buildings on such land as under all the circumstances of the case he may deem fair and reasonable:

3*rd*,—he may determine the amount of such compensation, notwithstanding that no person interested in such land has appeared before him in pursuance of the notice issued by him under s. 9 of the said Act;

4*th*,—when he has determined the amount of such compensation, he may take possession of the land, which shall thereupon vest absolutely in the Government free from all encumbrances;

5*th*,—on determining the amount of compensation, he may pay that amount to the persons whom he may deem entitled thereto; but nothing herein contained shall affect the liability of any person who may receive the whole or any part of such compensation to pay the same to the person lawfully entitled thereto;

6*th*,—sections 14 to 16 (both inclusive), ss. 18 to 23 (both inclusive), and ss. 26 to 42 (both inclusive) of the said Land Acquisition Act, 1870, shall not apply to the cases herein referred to:

7*th*,—except as hereinbefore provided, the provisions of that Act, so far as they may be applicable consistently with the provisions hereinbefore contained, shall apply to such cases."

By s. 107 any Revenue-officer by name or by office may be vested with any of the powers specified in Act X of 1870, s. 4.

BURMA.—By s. 80 of the *Burma Forest Act* (XIX of 1881 of the Supreme Legislative Council), "whenever it appears to the Chief Commissioner that any land is required for the purposes of this Act, such land shall be deemed to be needed for a public purpose within the meaning of the Land Acquisition Act, 1870, s. 4."

And by s. 12 of the same Act, power is given to acquire land for a reserved forest in or over which any right is claimed other than a right of way, a right to a water-course or the use of water, or a right of pasture or to forest produce. For the purpose of so acquiring such land, (i) the Forest Settlement-Officer shall be deemed to be a Collector proceeding under the Land Acquisition Act, 1870; (ii) the claimant shall be deemed to be a person interested and appearing before him in pursuance of a notice given under s. 9 of that Act; (iii) the provisions of the preceding sections of that Act shall be deemed to have been complied with; and (iv) the Collector, with the consent of the claimant, or the Court, with the consent of both parties, may award compensation in land, or partly in land and partly in money.

The *Burma Municipal Act* (XVII of 1884 of the Supreme Legislative Council) contains similar provisions to those contained in the Punjab Municipalities Act (noticed above), with this exception that under s. 38 land may be acquired not only when needed for the purposes of that Act, but also when required "for any other object which the Municipal Committee is empowered to carry out under any other enactment for the time being in force."

By Act XIX of 1884 (*Rangoon Waterworks*), s. 6, compensation for damage done in the construction or maintenance of the works is to be determined as nearly as may be in accordance with the provisions of the Land Acquisition Act.

BENGAL.—Part II of the *Bengal Irrigation Act*, III (B. C.) of 1876, treats of claims to compensation in respect of the application or use of the water of any natural stream or lake for the purpose of any existing or projected canal (s. 6). The procedure to be followed is very similar to that laid down in the Land Acquisition Act. Sections 8 to 10 relate to the issue of notices and the submission of claims to the Collector; and the only point worthy of notice is that the Collector may impose a daily fine for non-compliance with his requisition under s. 10.

Then s. 11 says :—

"No compensation shall be awarded for any damage caused by—

(*a*) stoppage or diminution of percolation, or floods ;

(*b*) deterioration of climate or soil ;

(*c*) stoppage of navigation, or of the means of rafting timber or watering cattle.

But compensation may be awarded in respect of any of the following matters :—

(*d*) stoppage or diminution of supply of water through any natural channel to any defined artificial channel, whether above or under ground, in use at the date of the issue of the notification under s. 6 :

(*e*) stoppage or diminution of supply of water to any work erected for purposes of profit on any channel, whether natural or artificial, in use at the date of the said notification :

(*f*) stoppage or diminution of supply of water through any natural channel which has been used for purposes of irrigation within the five years next before the date of the said notification :

(*g*) damage done in respect of any right to a water-course or the use of any water to which any person is entitled under the Indian Limitation Act, 1877, Part IV :

(*h*) any other substantial damage not falling under any of the above clauses (*a*), (*b*) or (*c*) and caused by the exercise of the powers conferred by this Act, which is capable of being ascertained and estimated at the time of awarding such compensation. Notwithstanding anything contained in cl. (*c*), compensation may be awarded in respect of the loss of any tolls which were lawfully levied on any river or channel at the time of the issue of the notification mentioned in s. 6.

In determining the amount of compensation under this section, regard shall be had to the diminution in the market-value at the time of awarding compensation of the property in respect of which compensation is claimed ; and where such market-value is not ascertainable, the amount shall be reckoned at twelve times the amount of the diminution of the annual nett profits of such property, caused by the exercise of the powers conferred by this Act.

Section 12 provides that if any supply of drinking water is substantially deteriorated or diminished by any works undertaken under the Act, the Canal Officer shall be bound to provide within convenient distance an adequate supply in lieu thereof, and no person shall be entitled to obtain any further compensation on that account. Section 13 provides that no claim for compensation for any stoppage, diminution or damage, shall be entertained after the expiration of six months from such stoppage, diminution or damage, unless the Collector is satisfied that the claimant had sufficient cause for not making the claim within such period. Sections 14—16 are the same as ss. 11, 12 and 14 of the Land Acquisition Act. Sections 17—19 correspond with s. 15 of the Land Acquisition Act, but they contain an important innovation.* Of the five cases in which the Collector is bound by s. 15

---

* On this matter the Select Committee reported as follows:—

" We have laid down more fully the procedure for settling claims to compensation for damage caused by the exercise of the powers of the Lieutenant-Governor (under ss. 6 and 7) of applying water to public purposes ; and in so doing, we have generally followed and adapted the procedure of the Land Acquisition Act of 1870, where of the Land Acquisition Act to make a reference to the Court, only the two last are provided for by s. 17 of the Bengal Irrigation Act. The second case mentioned in s. 15 of the Land Acquisition Act, namely, where the Collector considers that further enquiry as to the nature of the claim should be made by the Court, is not referred to in the Bengal Irrigation Act. The other two cases, *viz.*, where no claimant attends, and where a person whom the Collector has reason to think interested fails to attend, are thus provided for in ss. 18 and 19. The Collector is to hold a proceeding and record the following particulars :—

(*a*) the nature and extent of the property of which the value has been diminished and in respect of which compensation is claimed, and the character and extent of the damage done ;

(*b*) the names of the persons whom he has reason to think interested in such property ;

(*c*) the amount fixed by him as compensation ; and

(*d*) the grounds on which such amount was determined.

The amount so fixed is then to be placed in deposit on account of the persons interested, and a notice to be issued to them to the effect that if no application be made to the Court within six weeks of the issue of the notice, the amount will be paid to any persons legally authorized to receive and to give an acquittance for the same. If any application is made to the Court within the period stated, the Court is to proceed to determine the amount of compensation and all other matters as if a reference had been made to it by the Collector.

Section 20 corresponds with s. 18 of the Land Acquisition Act. Section 21 says :—

"On receipt of a reference under s. 17 the Court shall proceed, so far as may be practicable, in accordance with ss. 19 to 23 (inclusive) and ss. 26 to 36 (inclusive) of the Land Acquisition Act, 1870 ; provided that, instead of the last clause of the

---

applicable ; but in order to obviate an inconvenience which has been experienced in petty cases under that Act, we have provided that a reference shall not necessarily be made to the Civil Court in every case in which the applicants fail to appear to settle the amount of compensation with the Collector ; but that in such cases the Collector shall make an award, of which due notice shall be given, and which shall become final unless it is contested before the Civil Court within a specified time.

said s. 26, the following shall be read : 'The provisions of this section and of s. 11 of the Bengal Irrigation Act, 1876, shall be read to every assessor in a language which he understands, before he gives his opinion as to the amount of compensation to be awarded."

Sections 22 and 23 are the same as ss. 37 and 38 of the Land Acquisition Act; but the following important clause is added to the latter section :—

" All costs entailed by such a reference, and the proceedings of the Court thereon, shall be paid by the parties who dispute the apportionment of the compensation, in such proportions as the Court may direct, and the Collector shall not be required to disburse any such costs, nor shall any such costs be recovered from the Collector."

Sections 25 and 27 correspond with s. 40 of the Land Acquisition Act. Section 26 runs thus :—" The amount of compensation fixed by any award, proceeding or decision, as specified in the last preceding section, shall be deemed to be the full amount payable by the Government in respect of the claim dealt with therein; and the Government shall not be liable for any further claim to any person whatever in respect of any matter which was the subject of such award, proceeding or decision ; nor shall any such claim be made against the Government in respect of the payment of any portion of such compensation in accordance with any award, proceeding or decision as aforesaid, or in accordance with any decision of the Judge or of the District Judge or of the High Court in appeal, as the case may be, under s. 24 ; and no suit shall be brought to set aside an award or decision under this Act." It is to be observed that there is no provision in this Part of the Act corresponding with s. 42 of the Land Acquisition Act.

Sections 28 and 29 deal with questions of abatement of rent. Section 30 provides that the compensation shall become due three months after the claim is made, and if not paid shall carry interest at 6 per cent. per annum unless the non-payment is caused by the wilful neglect or refusal of the claimant to receive the same. The section also empowers the Collector to invest the amount in Government securities, in which case the claimant will only get the interest on such securities.

Section 31 provides that no compensation shall be claimable in respect of works executed before the Act came into force, or of any damage, injury or loss caused by such works.

The provisions of Part II of the Act are also extended by s. 44 to claims for compensation on account of loss consequent on the removal or modification of obstructions under s. 40, or the construction of a drainage work under s. 43.

By s. 52 land may be acquired under the Land Acquisition Act when any person desires the construction of a new village channel, but is unable or unwilling to construct it under a private arrangement with the owners and occupiers of the land affected.

In cases of entry upon land or buildings under ss. 7, 33, 34, 35 or 43, the Canal-officer or person making the entry is to ascertain and record the nature of any crop, tree, building or other property to which damage has been done, and the extent of the damage done to such property, and to tender compensation for the same. If the tender is not accepted, the Canal-officer is to refer the matter to the Collector, who will make enquiry and determine (subject to an appeal to the Commissioner) the amount of compensation.

Section 76, cl. (*b*), contains the following provisions in regard to compensation for the failure or stoppage of the water-supply from a canal :—

"No claim shall be made against the Government for compensation in respect of loss caused by the failure or stoppage of the water in a canal, by reason of any cause beyond the control of Government, or of any repairs, alterations or additions to the canal, or of any measures taken for regulating the proper flow of water therein, or for maintaining the established course of irrigation which the Canal-officer considers necessary; but the person suffering such loss shall be entitled to such remission of the ordinary charges payable for the use of the water as is authorized by the Lieutenant-Governor :

(*c*) " If the supply of water to any land irrigated from a canal be interrupted otherwise than in the manner described in the last preceding clause, the occupier or owner of such land may present a petition for compensation to the Collector for any loss arising from such interruption, and the Collector shall award to the petitioner reasonable compensation for such loss."

The provisions of the Land Acquisition Act are also extended by the *Bengal Drainage Act*, VI (B. C.) of 1880, to claims for compensation in respect of land taken for, or damage caused or likely to be caused by, the construction of any drainage works carried out under that Act.

Section 21 says :—" When the Lieutenant-Governor has sanctioned any scheme, plans and estimates as aforesaid, or some portion thereof, he may direct proceedings to be taken under the provisions of the Land Acquisition Act, 1870, or any other law for the time being in force for the acquisition of land for public purposes, in order to obtain any land likely to be required for the works mentioned in such sanctioned scheme, plans and estimates, or any portion thereof."

And s. 24 runs as follows :—

(1) "Any person who alleges that damage has been caused to his property by any scheme or works carried out under this Act may, at any time before the expiry of the three years mentioned in cl. (1) of s. 28, prefer to the Commissioners a claim for compensation in respect of such *damage actually caused* and of *all future damage likely to be caused* to such property by such scheme or works.

" The Commissioners shall duly consider any such claim; and if they are satisfied that such damage has been caused or is likely to be caused, they shall assess such compensation as to them appears fair and reasonable.

" If such person agrees to accept the amount so assessed, the same shall be paid to him; if he do not agree to accept such amount, the Commissioners shall make a reference to the Civil Court in the manner in which a Collector is empowered to make a reference by s. 15 of the Land Acquisition Act, 1870, and the provisions of Part III of the said Act shall apply to any reference so made.

(2) " When the persons interested in such property, to which damage has been caused as aforesaid, agree to accept the amount of compensation assessed by the Commissioners, but a dispute arises as to the apportionment of the same or any part thereof, or when the amount of compensation has been settled by the Court on a reference under cl. (1) of this section, and a similar dispute arises, the Commissioners shall refer such dispute to the

decision of the Civil Court, and the provisions of Part IV of the said Land Acquisition Act shall apply to any reference so made.

(3) "When the amount of compensation assessed by the Commissioners does not exceed one thousand rupees, any reference made under the said cl. (1) may be transferred by the Principal Civil Court of original jurisdiction of the district to any Subordinate Judge in the same district, and such Subordinate Judge shall have power to hear and dispose of the same; and any reference made under cl. (2) of this section may be transferred by such Principal Civil Court to any Munsif in the same district, and such Munsif shall have power to hear and dispose of the same."

Part V of the *Bengal Embankment Act*, II (B. C.) of 1882, treats of claims to compensation for land acquired or damage done in carrying out the provisions of that Act. The sections in question are given at length :—

Section 37.—" Whenever in the course of proceedings under this Act, save in those cases in which the Collector has proceeded under the provisions of ss. 12 and 13, Bengal Act VI of 1873, it appears that land is required for any of the purposes thereof, proceedings shall be forthwith taken for the acquisition of such land in accordance with the provisions of the Land Acquisition Act X of 1870, or other law for the time being in force for the acquisition of lands for public purposes."

Section 38.—" Subject to the provisions of s. 5, whenever any land other than land required or taken by the engineer, or any right of fishery, right of drainage, right of the use of water, or other right or property shall have been injuriously affected by any act done or any work executed under the due exercise of the powers or provisions of this Act, the person in whom such property or right is vested may prefer a claim by petition to the Collector for compensation : Provided that the refusal to execute any work for which application is made, and the refusal of permission to execute any work for the execution of which the permission of the Collector or any other authority is required under this Act, shall not be deemed acts on account of which a claim for compensation can be preferred under this section."

Section 39.—" No claim under the last preceding section shall be entertained which shall be made later than two years next after the completion of the work by which such right is injuriously affected."

Section 40.—" When any such claim is made, proceedings shall be taken in view to determine the amount of compensation, if any, which should be made, and the person to whom the same should be payable, as far as possible in accordance with the provisions of the Land Acquisition Act X of 1870, or other law for the time being in force for the acquisition of land for public purposes."

Section 41.—" In any such case which is referred to the Judge and Assessors for the purpose of determining whether any, and, if so, what amount of compensation should be awarded, the Judge and Assessors shall take into consideration—

First, the market-value of the property or right injuriously affected at the time when the act was done or the work executed.

Secondly, the damage sustained by the claimant by reason of such act or work injuriously affecting the property or right.

Thirdly, the consequent diminution of the market-value of the property or right injuriously affected, when the act was done or the work executed.

Fourthly, whether any person has derived, or will derive benefit from the act or work in respect of which the compensation is claimed or from any work connected therewith, in which case they shall set off the estimated value of such benefit, if any, against the compensation which would otherwise be decreed to such person.

But the Judge or Assessors shall not take into consideration,— first, the degree of urgency which has led to the act or work being done or executed ; secondly, any damage sustained by the claimant, which, if caused by a private person, would not in any suit instituted against such person justify a decree for damages."

Sections 12 and 13 of Bengal Act VI of 1873 (referred to in s. 37 above) refer to cases in which the Collector is of opinion that the delay in the execution of any work that would be caused by following the ordinary procedure for acquiring the land would be attended with grave and imminent danger to life or property (ss. 25 & 30). In such cases he may take immediate possession of the land, and may offer adequate compensation to the persons interested for the estimated value of the crops and trees, if any, standing on the land. If the offer is not accepted, the amount of compensation will be determined in accordance with the provisions of the Land Acquisition Act. (See Bengal Act VI of 1873, ss. 21, 26 and 29.) If, on the subsequent enquiry, it appears that anything done under s. 25 of Bengal Act II of 1882 was unnecessary, compensation is to be awarded under Part V of the Act, and the land or embankment or drainage is to be restored at the expense of Government as nearly as may be to the state in which it was before.

By s. 19 of the Act land may be acquired when it appears on enquiry that the removal of any trees, houses, huts or other buildings situated between a public embankment and the river is necessary, or that land is required for widening an existing embanked tow-path, or for constructing a new embanked tow-path. By ss. 34 — 36 when earth or other material is required to repair any embankment or water-course, or embanked tow-path maintained by Government, the Collector is to proceed in respect of any crops upon the land in the manner provided by s. 13, Bengal Act VI of 1873 (*supra*); but if the land is thereby rendered permanently unfit for cultivation, the Government must acquire the land under the Land Acquisition Act.

By s. 35 of the *Bengal Municipal Act*, III (B.C.) of 1884, the Local Government may, on the application of the Commissioners and on being satisfied that they are in a position to pay either at once or in such instalments as it thinks proper, acquire land for the Commissioners as for a public purpose, and on payment by them of the compensation awarded, the land will vest in them for the purposes of the Act. And the next section makes it incumbent on them to pay for the land so acquired on their behalf.

It remains to notice the provisions of the *Calcutta Municipal Consolidation Act*, 1889, recently passed by the Bengal Legislative Council in connection with this subject.

By s. 397 the Commissioners in meeting may acquire any land, whether within or without Calcutta, for any of the purposes of the Act, and may dispose of land vested in them, and the Commissioners may receive the rent of any land leased by them on such terms as they may think fit. By s. 398 the Commissioners in meeting may pay rent for, or take on lease, any land required for the purposes of the Act. And by s. 399 "any land required for the purposes of this Act may be acquired under the provisions of the Land Acquisition Act, 1870, or any similar Act for the time being in force for the acquisition of land for public purposes; and on payment by the Commissioners, out of the General Fund, of the compensation payable under that Act, and of the charges reasonably incurred by the Collector in respect of the proceedings thereunder, such land shall vest in them for the purposes of this Act."

Over and above these general powers, certain cases are specifically provided for by the Act in which the Commissioners are expressly authorized to acquire land. An example of this is to be found in s. 204, by which, as in the Bombay Municipal Act, the Commissioners in meeting are authorized to "acquire any land required for the purposes of opening, widening, extending or otherwise improving any public street or of making any new street, and the buildings, if any, standing upon such land:" and also to "acquire, in addition to such land and the buildings, if any, standing thereupon, all such land with the buildings, if any, standing thereupon, as it shall seem expedient to the Commissioners to acquire outside of the regular line of such street, provided that, without the special sanction of the Local Government, not more than one hundred feet shall be acquired on either side of the regular line of the street;" and the Commissioners are authorized to lease or sell or otherwise dispose of any land or building so purchased under such conditions as they think fit as to the removal of the existing building, the description of the new building to be erected, the period within which such new building shall be completed, and other such matters.

Similarly, under s. 261 the Commissioners are authorized to acquire any land other than bustee land shown in the report of the medical officers appointed to report on unhealthy bustees as land which should be acquired.

And by s. 268 the Commissioners in meeting may, with the sanction of the Local Government, acquire under the Act unhealthy bustees, and sell or lease or themselves improve the same.

It would appear that it is only when land is acquired under the Land Acquisition Act that the provisions of that Act will apply as to determining the amount of compensation. In other cases where compensation for damage done is payable by the Commissioners, a special procedure is laid down (ss. 423—426). The amount, and, if necessary, the apportionment of the same in case of dispute is to be ascertained and determined by a Court of Small Causes, and the amount so determined may be recovered by distress or by suit. In this manner, to instance a few examples, the compensation is in case of dispute to be settled for permanently closing and selling the site of the roadway or footpath of a street under s. 205 ; for setting back buildings to the regular line of the street under s. 207 ; or for removing existing projections from houses under s. 222. It may be mentioned that certain principles on which the compensation is to be assessed are laid down in ss. 205 and 207.

INDEX.

The figures given refer to the pages.

ABATEMENT
    of rent of land acquired, 71.
    of revenue, 90—94.

ACQUISITION, *see* LAND.
    notification of likelihood of, 18.
    declaration of intended, 19.
    Collector when to take order for, 21.
    Government not always bound to complete, 64.
    of land for Companies, 81.
    of mines, 103.

ACTION, *see* SUIT.

ACTS OF THE LEGISLATIVE COUNCILS.
    1839—XXVIII, 3.
    1850—I, 2.
    ——XVII, 3.
    ——XLII, 2, 29.
    1852—XX, 3.
    1854—I, 4.
    1857—VI, 4, 14, 15, 28, 32, 33, 34, 73, 85, 88.
    1858—XXXV, 17.
    ——XL, 17.
    1861—II, 5, 79, 80, 85.
    1863—XXII, 5, 83, 99—100.
    1865—I (Bombay), 94.
    1870—VII, 62.
    ——X, 6, 9—89.
    1871—VI, 72.
    ——VI (Madras), 113.
    ——IX, 89.
    ——XXXIII, 100, 122.
    1872—III (Bombay), 116.
    1873—VI (Bombay), 116.

1873—VI (Bengal), 132.
———VII (Bombay), 117.
———VIII, 120.
———XV, 121.
1876—III (Bengal), 20, 65, 125.
———VIII (Bengal), 91.
———XII, 63.
1877—XV, 63, 76, 80, 85, 89.
1878—V (Bombay), 117.
1879—VI (Bombay), 117.
——— VII (Bombay), 117.
———XIII, 16.
1880—VI (Bengal), 16, 130.
1881—XVIII, 100, 122.
———XIX, 124.
1882—I (Madras), 113.
——— V (Madras), 113.
———II (Bengal), 131.
1883—XIV, 122.
———XV, 122.
1884—I (Madras), 114.
———IV (Madras), 115.
———V (Madras), 115.
———VI (Madras), 115.
———XIII, 122.
———XVII, 125.
———XVIII, 16.
———XIX, 125.
———III (Bengal), 133.
1885—XVIII, 8, 15, 29, 97—111.
1886—II (Madras), 115.
———IV (Madras), 115.
———XI, 20.
———XX, 16.
1887—XII, 72.

ADDING
 parties, provisions of Code of Civil Procedure applicable, 63.

ADDITIONAL COMPENSATION
 for compulsory acquisition, 76.

ADDITIONS
   to rules under Act, 89.

ADJOURNMENT,
   provisions of Code of Civil Procedure applicable, 64.

AGENTS
   authorized to receive service, 22.

AGREEMENT
   for the temporary occupation of land, 79.
   to be entered into by Company, 82.
   declaration not to issue till agreement has been executed, 81.
   to be published in *Gazettes*, 83.
   not chargeable with stamp-duty and no fee for copy, 87.

AJMIR
   Land and Revenue Regulation II of 1877, 100, 123.

ALTERATIONS
   of rules under Act, 89.

AMENDS,
   tender of, for act done in pursuance of Act, 88.

AMOUNT
   of compensation, *see* COMPENSATION.
   awarded, *see* AWARD.
   tendered, *see* TENDER.

APPEAL,
   no appeal from opinion of Judge on question of law, 58.
   no appeal when Judge agrees with one or both of assessors as to amount of compensation, 59.
   but when Judge differs from both assessors, his decision is open to appeal, 62.
   to what Court appeal lies, 62.
   time and manner of appeal, 62.
   appeal from Judge's decision as to apportionment, 65.
   payment according to decision on appeal, 73.
   but not to be made pending appeal, 77.

APPOINTMENT
   of special officer as Collector, 16.
   of special officer as Judge, 16.
   of assessors, 31—35.

APPOINTMENT—(*Continued.*)
    of officer to hold enquiry under s. 48, p. 82.
    of officer to inspect mines, 103, 108.
        see GOVERNMENT, OFFICER OF.

APPORTIONMENT
    where parties are agreed, may be specified in award, 64.
    dispute to be referred to Court, 65.
    to be decided by Judge sitting alone, 65.
    principles of, 66.

ARABLE LAND,
    immediate possession of, 29.
    may be occupied temporarily, 78.

AREA
    to be stated in declaration, 19.
    to be ascertained by Collector, 21.
    to be stated in notice, 21, and in reference, 30.

ASSESSOR
    by whom to be nominated, 31.
    in case of failure to nominate, 32.
    to determine amount of compensation, 33.
    appointment of new assessor in case of death, refusal, neglect or incapability, 35.
    powers of new assessor, 35.
    matters which assessors are to take into consideration, 36.
    matters which they are not to take into consideration, 53.
    ss. 24—26 to be read to assessors, 58.
    opinion to be given orally and recorded by Judge, 58.
    difference of opinion between Judge and assessor on point of law, 58.
    when Judge and assessors agree as to compensation, 59.
    when they differ, 60.
    non-official assessor to receive fee, 60.
    to sign award in which he concurs, 61.

ATTENDANCE
    of witnesses, *see* WITNESSES.
    of persons interested, 23, 25.

AWARD
    may be made by Collector if all agree, 24.
    to be conclusive evidence between Collector and persons interested, 24.

AWARD—(*Continued.*)
    in case of dispute, to be determined by Judge and assessors, 31.
    matters for which compensation may be awarded, 36.
    matters for which compensation may not be awarded, 53.
    limits of award, 57.
    award final in certain cases, 59.
    but not where Judge differs from both assessors, 60.
    to be in writing, signed by Judge and assessor concurring, to specify items of compensation separately and amount of costs, 61.
    to specify particulars of apportionment, 64.
    payment to be made to person named in award, 73.
    award to be followed by payment and possession, 75.
    after award Government bound to complete acquisition, 84.
    not liable to stamp-duty, 87.
    not liable to be set aside by suit, 88.

BANKRUPTCY
    of parties, Code of Civil Procedure applicable, 64.

BENGAL
    Government rules under s. 59, pp. 90—93.
    cognate Acts of Bengal Council, 125.
        see ACTS.

BOMBAY,
    surrender of possession how enforceable in, 84.
    former law in, 3.
    Government rules under s. 59, pp. 94-95.
    cognate Acts of Bombay Council, 116.
        see ACTS.

BORE,
    power to, 18.

BOUNDARIES
    may be set out in preliminary survey, 18.
    penalty for displacing, 84.

BRITISH BURMA,
    definition of Court in, 16.
    cognate Acts relating to, 124.

BRITISH INDIA,
    Act extends to whole of, 13.

BUILDING
   not to be entered without notice, 18.
   part only not to be taken, 85.

CALCUTTA,
   surrender of possession how enforceable in, 84.
   Municipal Consolidation Act, 1889, 133—5.

CHANGE
   of residence, expenses of, 36.

CLAIM
   to be invited by Collector, 21.
   to be invited by Court, if not made before Collector, 30.
   may be referred to Court, 25.
   refusal or omission to make claim, 58.
   amount awarded not to exceed claim, 57.

CLAIMANT, *see* PERSON INTERESTED.

CODE OF CIVIL PROCEDURE,
   made applicable to summoning witnesses by Collector, 23.
   applicable to proceedings before Court, 63.
   to regulate appeal as to compensation, 63.
   to regulate appeal as to apportionment, 66.
   made applicable to enquiry into utility of work projected by Company, 82.

CODE PENAL, *see* INDIAN PENAL CODE.

COLLECTOR,
   definition of, 16.
   to give notice that land is likely to be required, 18.
   to assess damage in preliminary survey, 19.
   to take order for acquisition, 21.
   to cause land to be marked out and measured, 21.
   to give general and special notice, 21.
   empowered to call for statement of interests, 22.
   to enquire into value and claims and to make a tender, 23.
   empowered to enforce attendance of witnesses, &c., 23.
   may postpone enquiry, 24.
   to be guided by ss. 24-25, p. 24.
   may make award if all agree, 24.
   when to refer the matter to Court, 25.

COLLECTOR—(*Continued.*)
    when empowered to take possession, 28.
    when in case of urgency, 29.
    to offer compensation for crops and trees, 29.
    what statement to make to Court, 30.
    to nominate assessor, 31.
    to advance all costs under Part III, 60.
    when to pay costs, 61.
    when may appeal against award, 62.
    to refer dispute as to apportionment to Court, 65.
    to pay persons named in award, 73.
    when to pay, 75, 77.
    to pay additional compensation, 76.
    when to pay interest, 76.
    empowered to procure the temporary occupation of land, 78.
    to refer disagreement as to compensation to Court, 79.
    when to take possession, 79.
    to restore possession, 80.
    to refer disputes to Court, 81.
    notices to be signed by or by order of, 83.
    how to get possession if opposed, 84.
    to determine compensation when acquisition is not completed, 84.
    to recover costs from Municipal fund or Company, 87.
    may abstain from acquiring mines, 101.
    may apply Mines Act to pending cases, 110.

COMMISSION,
    to examine absent witnesses, 64.
    to make local enquiry, 64.

COMMISSIONER
    of Division included in definition of Court, 16.
    of Police to enforce surrender of possession, 84.
        see DEPUTY COMMISSIONER.

COMMITTEE
    of lunatic entitled to act, 17.

COMPANY,
    definition of, 17.
    definition of, under Mines Act, 110.

COMPANY—(*Continued.*)

declaration may issue when compensation is payable by, 19.
after consent of Government and agreement, 81.
to execute agreement with Secretary of State, 82.
officer of, may be authorized to enter and survey, 81.
may acquire temporary use of land, 78.
to pay Collector's charges, 87.
application of Mines Act to land transferred to, 109.

COMPENSATION

for damage done in preliminary survey, 19.
for crops and trees in case of immediate possession, 29.
for land acquired—claim may be made to Collector, 21.
who may determine amount, 23.
and award it if all agree, 24.
if not, must refer matter to Court, 25.
in which case claim may be made to Court, 30.
to be determined by Judge and assessors, 33.
matters for which compensation will be allowed, 36.
matters for which compensation will not be allowed, 53.
limits of, 57.
award when final, 59.
when not final, 60.
items to be specified separately in award, 6.
apportionment of, 64—72.
payment of, to whom, 73.
when, 75, 77.
for temporary occupation and use of land, 78.
and for damage done thereto, 79.
when acquisition is not completed, 84.
for mines or minerals, 103.
how to be ascertained, 104.
for injury done to mines, 107.
for injury done to adjacent surface, 108.

COMPULSORY ACQUISITION,

additional compensation for, 76.

CONCLUSIVE, *see* EVIDENCE.

CONDITION

of land on expiry of occupation, 81.

CONDITIONS
on which work shall be executed and maintained, 82.

CONSENT
of occupier to enter building, 18.
of Local Government to acquisition by Company, 81.

CONSTRUCTION
of work of public utility, 82.

CO-PROPRIETOR,
statement of interest of, 22.
see PERSON INTERESTED.

COPY
of notice, how to be served, 83.
of award or agreement to be given free of charge, 87.

COSTS
to include assessor's fees, 60.
to be advanced by Collector, 60.
by which party to be ultimately paid, 60.
to be stated in award, and by what persons and in what proportions they are to be paid, 61.
may be deducted from amount awarded, 77.
or levied as costs in suit, 61.
may be recovered from Municipal Fund or Company, 87.

COURT,
definition, 16.
Local Government may appoint special Judge, 16.
reference to Court as to compensation for land acquired and questions of title, 25.
statement of reference what to contain, 30.
to serve notices, 30.
Judge to appoint assessor on failure of nomination, 32.
to determine compensation with aid of assessors, 33.
to substitute assessor, 35.
matters to be considered by Judge and assessors, 36.
matters to be neglected, 53.
Judge to decide as to sufficiency of reason for omitting to make claim, 58.
to record opinions of assessors, 58.
opinion of Judge to prevail on points of law, 58.

COURT—(*Continued.*)
    decision when final, 59.
    in case of disagreement Judge's decision to prevail, 60.
    subject to appeal, 62.
    Judge to fix assessor's fees, 60.
    award to be signed by Judge and assessor concurring, 61.
    persons interested to appear in, 31.
    proceedings to be in open Court, 35.
    reference to Court as to apportionment, 65.
    Judge sitting alone to decide, 65.
    subject to appeal, 65.
    reference as to compensation for temporary use of land, 79.
    or as to condition of land on expiry of term, 81.
    Judge sitting alone to decide, 81.

CROP
    may be cut in preliminary survey, 18.
    compensation to be given for, 29.

DAMAGE
    in preliminary survey to be assessed by Collector, 19.
    by severance, compensation for, 36.
    by injurious affecting of other property or earnings, 36.
    non-actionable not to be compensated, 53.
    prospective not to be compensated, 53.
    to land temporarily occupied, compensation for, 80.
    when acquisition is not completed, 84.
    to surface by improper working of mines, 105.
    by reason of severance of mines, 107.
    to land lying over mines, 108.

DAMAGES, *see* AMENDS.

DAMAGING
    trench or mark made punishable, 84.

DEATH
    of parties—Code of Civil Procedure applicable, 64.
    of assessor, 35.

DECLARATION
    that land is likely to be needed, 18.
    of intended acquisition, 19.
    that mines are not needed, 101.

DECREE,
   costs may be recovered as if under, 61.
DEPRECIATION, *see* DAMAGE.
DEPUTY COMMISSIONER
   included in definition of Collector, 16.
DESTROYING
   trench or mark made punishable, 84.
DETERMINATION OF AMOUNT OF COMPENSATION
   by Collector, 23.
   when to be referred to Court, 25.
   assessors to be nominated to aid Judge, 30.
   by Judge and assessors, 33.
   matters to be considered, 36.
   matters to be neglected, 53.
   for mines, 104, 108.
DIFFERENCE, *see* DISPUTE.
DIG,
   power to, 18.
DISABILITY, *see* INCAPABILITY.
DISCHARGE
   of assessor, 35.
DISINCLINATION
   to sell not to be taken into consideration, 53.
DISPLACING
   trench or mark made punishable, 84.
DISPUTE
   as to damage done in survey, 19.
   as to compensation or title before Collector, 25.
   as to value of crops or trees, 29.
   between Judge and assessors as to compensation, 60.
   as to apportionment, 65.
   as to compensation for land temporarily occupied, 79.
   as to condition of land on expiry of agreement, 81.
   or as to any matter connected with agreement, 81.
DISTRICT
   to be stated in declaration, 19.

DOCUMENTS,
production may be compelled by Collector, 23.
provisions of Code of Civil Procedure applicable, 64.
production may be compelled by officer holding enquiry under s. 48, p. 82.

DWELLING-HOUSE, *see* House.

EARNINGS,
loss of, to be compensated, 36.

ENCUMBRANCES,
statement of, 22.
land acquired free of, 28, 29.

ENHANCE, *see* Improvements.

ENTITLED
to act, definition of persons, 17.
to compensation, may recover from recipient, 73.

ENQUIRY
by Collector into value and claims, 23.
may be postponed, 24.
Collector may refer claim to Court for, 25.
when land is required by a Company, 82.
commission for local, 64.

EVIDENCE,
declaration to be conclusive, 19.
award to be conclusive, as to value, 24.
and as to correctness of apportionment, 64.

EXAMINATION
of parties and witnesses, Code of Civil Procedure applicable, 64.

EXTENT, *see* Area.

FAILURE
to nominate assessor, 32.
of assessor to act, 35.
to appoint new assessor, 35.

FEE,
non-official assessor to receive fee, to be fixed by Judge, not to exceed Rs. 500, to be costs in proceedings, 60.
no fee to be charged for copy of award or agreement, 87.

FENCE
may be cut for preliminary survey, 18.

FILLING
trench made punishable, 84.

FINE
for intentional omission to furnish statement, 23.
for wilful obstruction or mischief, 84.
for refusal to allow inspection of mines, 109.

GARDEN, *see* HOUSE.

"GAZETTE OF INDIA,"
agreement between Government and Company to be published in, 83.

GAZETTE, LOCAL,
publication of notification that land is likely to be needed, 18.
publication of declaration that land is needed, 19.
publication of agreement with Company, 83.
publication of rules, 89.
publication of extension of Mines Act, 99.

GOVERNMENT
may appoint special Judge, 16.
may notify that land is likely to be needed, 18.
may authorize preliminary survey, 18.
may declare that land is needed, 19.
may acquire land for a public purpose or for a Company, 19.
may direct Collector to take order for acquisition, 21.
may direct Collector to take immediate possession, 29.
may direct Collector to procure land for temporary occupation and use, 78.
to acquire such land if required to do so, 80.
may authorize officer of Company to exercise certain powers, 81.
previous consent necessary before land is acquired for a Company, 81.
to direct enquiry as to utility of work and necessity of acquisition, 82.
to require agreement from Company, 82.
not bound to complete acquisition unless award has been made or reference directed, 84.
may make rules under Act, 89.

GOVERNMENT—(*Continued.*)
rights to mines and minerals not affected, 100.
may declare that mines and minerals are not required, 101.
may cause mines to be inspected, 103, 108.
may prevent or restrict working of mines, 103.
may repair damage or remove obstruction, 105.
must pay compensation if working prevented or restricted, 103.
and for injury done to mines, 107.
and for injury to surface lands, 108.
may take measures to ensure safety of surface, 109.

GOVERNMENT, OFFICER OF,
may be specially appointed to perform functions of Collector, 16.
or of Judge, 16.
may be authorized to survey, 18.
to pay for damage, 18.
may sign declaration if authorized to certify orders of Government, 19.
may be authorized to direct Collector to take order for acquisition, 21.
not to receive fee as assessor, 60.
may be appointed to enquire into utility of work proposed by Company, 82.
to report result of enquiry to Government, 82.

GOVERNOR-GENERAL IN COUNCIL
may prescribe rules for the acquisition of land by Companies, 81.
may prescribe rules for agreement with Companies, 82.
to sanction rules having the force of law, 89.
may prescribe the manner of publishing statement under s. 3 of Mines Act, 102.
or declaration under s. 5, p. 103.
may prescribe dimensions of air-ways, &c. in mines, 107.

GROUND, *see* LAND.

GROUNDS
of Collector's valuation, 30.
of award, 61.

GUARDIAN,
entitled to act, 17.

HOUSE
not to be entered without notice, 18.
part only not to be acquired, 85.

IMMOVEABLE
property, injury to, 36.

IMPEDING
Collector in taking possession, *see* OBSTRUCTION, REFUSAL.

IMPRISONMENT
for wilful omission to supply statement, 23.
for filling trenches or destroying landmarks, 84.

IMPROVEMENTS
in anticipation of acquisition, 53.

INCAPABILITY
of persons interested, 17.
of assessor, 35.

INCREASE
in value, prospective, 53.

INDIAN PENAL CODE,
sections 175—176 made applicable, 23.

INJURIOUSLY AFFECTED, *see* DAMAGE.

INSOLVENCY
of parties, Code of Civil Procedure applicable, 64.

INSPECTION
of plan to be allowed, 19.
of mines, 103, 108.

INTEREST
on compensation from date of possession, 76.
in land, *see* PERSON INTERESTED.

JUDGE, *see* COURT.

JUNGLE
may be cut for preliminary survey, 18.

LAND,
definition, 14.
power to survey land likely to be needed, 18.
declaration of intended acquisition, 19.

LAND—(*Continued.*)

only to be made if land is to be paid for out of public or Municipal funds or by Company, 19.
after declaration land to be marked out and measured, 21.
notice of intended acquisition to be given on or near the land by Collector, 21.
statement of interests in the land, 22.
summary enquiry into value, 23.
reference in case of dispute as to title, 25.
when possession may be taken, 28.
in case of urgency, 29.
situation and extent to be noted in Collector's statement on reference to Court, 30.
in case of non-attendance of persons interested before Collector, Court to affix notice on or near the land, 31.
market-value to be awarded, and damage for severance or injurious affection, 36.
but other matters not to be taken into consideration in determining amount of compensation, *viz.*, (1) urgency of acquisition, (2) disinclination to sell, (3) non-actionable damage, (4) prospective damage, (5) prospective appreciation of land acquired, or (6) of other land, (7) outlay or improvements with object of enhancing compensation, 53.
temporary occupation and use of waste or arable land, 78.
when possession of such land may be taken, 79.
restoration on expiry of term, 80.
dispute as to condition of land on expiry of term, 81.
acquisition of land for Companies, 81—83.
Government not bound to complete acquisition, 84.
mines or minerals lying under land need not be taken, 101.
see MINES.

LANGUAGE

in which rules shall be read to assessors, 58.

LAW

point, Judge's opinion to prevail on, 58.

LEGALLY BOUND,

persons required to make statements, 23.

LEVELS

may be taken in preliminary survey, 18.

LIABILITY
of person required to deliver statement, 23.
of recipient of compensation, 73.
of person obstructing or displacing landmarks, 84.
of person refusing to allow inspection of mines, 109.

LINE
may be laid down in preliminary survey, 18.

LOCAL
authority, definition of, 110.
authority, application of Mines Act to land transferred to, 109.
enquiry, commission for, 64.
extent of Act, 13.
extent of Mines Act, 99.

LOCAL GAZETTE, see GAZETTE.

LOCAL GOVERNMENT, see GOVERNMENT.

LOSS
of earnings to be compensated, 36.

LUNATIC,
committee of, entitled to act, 17.

MADRAS,
surrender of possession how enforceable in, 84.
former law in Presidency, 3.
cognate Acts of Madras Council, 113.
   see ACTS.

MAGISTRATE
may convict for obstructing or destroying landmarks, 84.
may enforce surrender of land, 84.

MANUFACTORY,
part only not to be taken, 85.

MAP, *see* PLAN.

MARKET-VALUE
at time of awarding compensation to be considered, 36.
percentage on, to be paid by Collector in consideration of compulsory nature of acquisition, 76.

MARKS,
    power to place, 18.
    Collector to place, 21.
    displacement of, made punishable, 84.

MARRIAGE
    of parties, Code of Civil Procedure applicable, 64.

MARRIED WOMAN
    entitled to act, 17.

MATERIALS
    taken from land temporarily occupied, 78.

MEASUREMENT
    Collector to make, 21.

MINERALS, *see* MINES.

MINES,
    English rule as to, 15.
    Land Acquisition (Mines) Act, 97—111.
    right of Government in mines saved, 100.
    declaration that mines are not needed, 101.
    notice to be given before working mines, 102.
    power to prevent or restrict working, 103.
    mode of determining compensation, 104.
    if compensation is not given, may be worked in a proper manner, 104.
    communications in mines, 107.
    compensation for injury by severance, 107.
    compensation to surface owner, 108.
    power to inspect, 108.
    penalty for refusal to allow inspection, 109.
    if worked improperly, power to make safe the surface, 109.
    application of Mines Act to pending cases, 110.

MINORS,
    guardians of, entitled to act, 17.

MORTGAGEE,
    statement of interest of, 22.
        see PERSON INTERESTED.

MOVEABLE
    property, injury to, 36.

MUNICIPAL FUND,
    declaration may issue when compensation is payable from, 19.
    Collector's charges to be defrayed from, 87.

NAMES
    of persons interested to be stated, 22.
    on reference to Court, 30.

NEGLECT
    to appoint assessor, 32.
    to make claim, 58.
    on part of assessor to act, 35.

NOMINATION
    of assessors, 31—35.

NON-ACTIONABLE
    damage to be neglected, 53.

NON-ATTENDANCE
    of person interested before Collector, 24, 25, 31.

NON-REGULATION PROVINCES,
    definition of Court in, 16.

NOTICE
    that land is likely to be needed, 18.
    before entry of building, &c., 18.
    of intended acquisition, general and special, 19.
    by Court to make claim and appoint assessor, 30.
    to be affixed on land in certain cases, 31.
    of purpose for which land is temporarily needed, 78.
    to acquire land temporarily occupied, 80.
    mode of service of, 83.
    to take the whole of a house, manufactory or building, 85.
    of suit for anything done in pursuance of Act, 88.
    of intention to work mines, 102.

NOTIFICATION
    that land is likely to be needed, 18.
    that land is needed, 19.
    of agreement between Government and a Company, 83.
    of rules under Act, 89.

OBSTRUCTION
    to authorized acts made punishable, 84.
    in taking possession, 84.
    by improper working of mines, 105.
    in inspection of mines, 109.

OCCUPATION,
    occupant may remain in, till land is needed, 75.
    of land temporarily, 78.

OCCUPIER
    of building to have notice of entry, 18.
    of land acquired may remain in possession, 75.
        see PERSON INTERESTED.

OFFER, *see* TENDER.

OFFICER OF COMPANY, *see* COMPANY.

OFFICER OF GOVERNMENT, *see* GOVERNMENT, OFFICER OF.

OMISSION
    to nominate assessor, 32.
    to appoint new assessor, 35.
    to make claim, 58.

OPINION
    of assessor, 58.
    of Judge on question of law, 58.
    of Judge as to amount of compensation, 60.

OPPOSITION, *see* OBSTRUCTION.

OUTLAY
    in anticipation of acquisition, 53.

OWNER
    may require Government to take an entire building, 85.
        see PERSON INTERESTED.

PARTICULARS
    of land, 21.
    of claim, 22, 31.
    of apportionment, 64.

PARTIES,
    provisions as to adding, 63.
    death, marriage or insolvency of, 64.
    examination of, 64.
        see PERSON INTERESTED.

INDEX.

PAYMENT
    for damage in preliminary survey, 19.
    for crops and trees when immediate possession is taken, 29.
    amount paid to be entered in statement of reference, 30.
    of costs in determining compensation by Court, 60-61.
    of compensation to persons named in award, 73.
    on making award, 75.
    of additional compensation, 76.
    of interest, 76.
    in appealable cases, 77.
    of compensation for temporary use and occupation, 78.
    of damage not provided for by agreement, 79.
    of compensation when land is acquired for a Company, 82.
    of Collector's charges when land is acquired for a Municipality or a Company, 87.
    no land to be acquired under the Act unless payment is to be made out of public revenues, a Municipal fund, or by a Company, 19.

PENAL CODE, *see* INDIAN PENAL CODE.

PENALTY
    for omission to file statement, 23.
    for obstruction, &c., 84.
    for refusal to allow inspection of mines, 109.

PERMANENT
    unfitness of land after use, 80.

PERSON INTERESTED,
    definition, 15.
    includes owner, occupier, co-proprietor, sub-proprietor, mortgagee, tenant and others, 22.
    and owner, occupier and lessee of mines, 104.
    notice to appear before Collector and make claim, 21.
    Collector empowered to call for statement of persons interested, 22.
    non-attendance of, 24, 25, 31.
    Collector may make award if all agree, 24.
    but must refer to Court in case of disagreement, non-attendance, or dispute as to rights, 25.
    to be named in Collector's statement on reference, 30.
    to be served with notice by Court to make claim and to appoint assessor, 30.

PERSON INTERESTED —(*Continued.*)
 to have compensation for damage by severance, or injurious affecting of other property or earnings and costs of compulsory removal, 36.
 but not for disinclination to sell, non-actionable or prospective damage, &c., 53.
 limits of compensation when claim has been made and in case of omission, 57.
 in what case to pay costs, 60.
 how costs to be recovered, 61.
 when may appeal, 62.
 apportionment of compensation, when persons agree, 64.
 in case of dispute, 65.
 entitled to compensation for damage done in preliminary survey, 19.
 and for crops and trees, 29.
 in land temporarily occupied to have notice and to be entitled to compensation for use and occupation, 78.
 and for damage, 80.
 and may require Government to acquire it permanently, 80.
 disputes as to condition of land, 81.

PLAN
 to be made by Collector, 21.
 to be open to inspection, 19.

POSSESSION,
 notice that Government intends to take, 21.
 when Collector may take, 28.
 when in case of urgency, 29.
 Collector may allow occupants to remain in, 75.
 interest to be calculated from date of taking, 76.
 when Collector may take, of land needed for temporary use and occupation, 79.
 mode of enforcing surrender of, 84.

POST,
 when notice may be sent by, 22.

POSTPONEMENT
 of enquiry, s. 24, *see* ADJOURNMENT.

POWER
 to enter and survey land and take levels, 18.
 to dig or bore, &c., 18.

POWER—(*Continued.*)
    to set out boundaries and line and to mark them, 18.
    to clear land, 18.
    to acquire the land after declaration, 19.
    of Collector to require statement of persons interested, 22.
    to summon and enforce the attendance of witnesses, 23.
    to postpone enquiry, 24.
    to take possession, 25.
    to take immediate possession in case of urgency, 26.
    of Judge to appoint assessor, 32.
    to appoint new assessors, 35.
    to occupy land temporarily, 78.
    of Company to enter and survey, 81.
    of Magistrate to enforce surrender of possession, 84.
    to inspect the working of mines, 103, 108.
        see GOVERNMENT, COLLECTOR, COURT.

POWERS
    of new assessor, 35.

PRACTICE,
    Judge to decide question of, 58.

PROCEEDINGS
    before Collector, 23—25.
    before Court, 30—63.
    in apportionment cases, 65.
    in enquiry under s. 48, p. 82.
    certain provisions of Code of Civil Procedure made applicable, 63.
    no proceedings to be commenced for anything done in pursuance of the Act without notice, 88.

PRODUCTION OF DOCUMENTS,
    Code of Civil Procedure applicable on enquiry by Collector, 23.
    in proceedings before Court, 64.
    in enquiry under s. 48, p. 82.

PROFITS,
    Collector may call for statement of, 22.
        see EARNINGS.

PROSPECTIVE DAMAGE, *see* DAMAGE.

PUBLIC,
    terms on which the public may use a Company's work, 82.

PUBLICATION
    of notification that land is likely to be needed, 18.
    of declaration that land is needed, 19.
    of general notice on or near the land, 21, 31.
    of agreement with Company, 53.
    of rules framed under the Act, 89.

PUBLIC NOTICE, *see* NOTICE.

PUBLIC PURPOSE,
    land likely to be needed for, 18.
    land needed for, 19.

PUBLIC REVENUES,
    land to be paid for out of, may be acquired under Act, 19.

PUBLIC UTILITY,
    Government to be satisfied that work is of, 82.

PUTNIDAR
    when entitled to compensation, 67.

QUALIFIED
    assessor, 32.

REFERENCE TO COURT,
    when to be made, 25.
    possession may be taken after reference, 28.
    what statement necessary, 30.
    in dispute as to apportionment, 65.
    to be tried by Judge alone, 65.
    as to sufficiency of compensation for land temporarily occupied, 79.
    possession may be taken after reference, 79.
    as to condition of land on expiration of term, 81.
    as to any matter connected with agreement, 81.
    Government bound to complete acquisition after reference, 84.

REFERENCES
    to Acts repealed, 14.

REFUSAL
    of assessor to act, 35.
    to allow inspection of mines, 109.

REGULATION
    I of 1824, summary of, 1.
    XIX of 1814, 91.
    Provinces, definition of Court in, 16.

REMISSION, *see* ABATEMENT.
RENTS,
    Collector may call for statement of, 22.
REPEAL
    of Acts, 14.
RESIDENCE,
    expenses of change of, 36.
RESTORATION
    of land after temporary occupation, 79.
REVENUE, *see* ABATEMENT.
RIGHT
    of occupancy, *see* RYOT.
    of way, land acquired free from, 28.
RIGHTS,
    question as to rights to be referred to Court, 27.
RULES
    for determining compensation, 36—58.
    for acquisition of land for Companies, 81.
    for agreements with Companies, 82.
    for enforcing the provisions of the Act, 89.
    of Government, 91—95.
RYOT
    with right of occupancy entitled to compensation, 70.
SECRETARY
    to Government to sign declaration, 19.
    of State, Company to execute agreement with, 82.
SERVANTS
    of authorized officer may enter and survey, 18.
SERVICE
    of notices by Collector, 21.
    of notices by Court, 30.
    mode of, 83.
    on authorized agents, 22.
    of notice regarding land needed temporarily, 78.
SEVERANCE,
    damage by, *see* DAMAGE.

SIGNATURE
    of Secretary to declaration, 19.
    of Judge and assessors to award, 61.
    by or by order of Collector or Judge, 83.

SINDH,
    definition of Court in, 16.

SITUATION
    of land, 19, 30.

STAMP-DUTY
    not chargeable on statement of claim, award or agreement, 87.

STATEMENT
    on reference to Court, 30.
    of persons interested, 22.

SUB-PROPRIETOR,
    statement of interest of, 22.

SUBSOIL,
    power to bore into, 18.

SUFFICIENCY
    of compensation, *see* COMPENSATION, DAMAGE.

SUIT,
    costs may be recovered as if costs in, 61.
    appeal to be presented as if appeal in, 63, 66.
    no suit to set aside award, 88.
    no suit to be commenced without notice, 88.
    no compensation for damage which would not render private person liable to suit, 53.

SUMMONS,
    Collector may issue, 23.
    provisions of Code of Civil Procedure made applicable, 63.
    may be issued by officer holding enquiry under s. 48, p. 82.

SURRENDER
    of possession, how to be enforced, 84.

SURVEY,
    power to make preliminary survey, 18.

TEMPORARY
    occupation and use of land, 78.

TENANT,
> statement of interest of, 22.
> with right of occupancy, 70.

TENDER
> of compensation for damage done in survey, 19.
> for land to be acquired, 23.
> to be mentioned in Collector's statement of reference, 30.
> when award may or may not exceed, 57.
> costs to depend thereon, 60.
> for damage to land temporarily occupied not provided for by agreement, 80.
> of amends for anything done in pursuance of Act, 88.

TERMS
> on which land may be held by Company, 82.
> on which public may use the work, 82.
> agreement as to, to have the force of law, 83.

TERRITORIAL
> division to be stated in declaration, 19.

TIME
> for notice of entry into building, 17.
> enquiry not to be less than 15 days after notice, 22.
> possession after 15 days' notice, 29.
> for appeal under s. 35, p. 63.
> for appeal under s. 39, p. 66.
> for payment of compensation, 75, 76.
> for which land may be temporarily occupied, 78.
> for enquiry as to projected work by Company, 82.
> within which Company to execute work, 82.

TITLE,
> reference on question respecting, 25.
> of Government in land acquired, 28, 29.
> statement of interests, 22.
> decision on questions of, 65.
> of Company in land acquired, 82.
>> *see* ENTITLED, PERSON INTERESTED.

TRANSFER
> of land to Company, 82.

TREES,
  compensation to be given for, 29.

TRENCH
  may be cut in preliminary survey, 18.
  penalty for filling in, 84.

TRUSTEES
  entitled to act, 17.

UNFITNESS
  of land for former purpose, 80.

URGENCY,
  possession in case of, 29.

USAGE,
  Judge to decide question of, 58.

USE
  of land temporarily, 78.

UTILITY
  of work, enquiry as to, 82.

VALUATION
  of damage done in survey, 19.
  of land by Collector, 23.
  by Court, 33.
  of land required for temporary occupation, 78, 81.
  of crops and trees, 29.
  of damage when acquisition is not completed, 84.

VALUE,
  Collector's enquiry into, 23.
  prospective increase to, 53.
  of crops and trees to be allowed, 29.

VEST,
  land to, free of incumbrances, 28, 29.

WASTE
  land may be occupied temporarily, 78.
  immediate possession may be taken in case of urgency, 29.

WITNESSES,
>   attendance may be enforced by Collector, 23.
>   provisions of Code of Civil Procedure applicable to, 64.
>   attendance may be enforced by person holding enquiry under s. 48, p. 82.

WORK
>   of public utility, 82.
>   line of, may be set out, 18.

WORKMEN
>   of authorized officer may enter and survey, 18.

WRITING,
>   notice under s. 4 to be in, 18.
>   notice under s. 43 to be in, 78.
>   notice of intention to work mines to be in, 102.

LAND AND REVENUE SALE-LAW.

The Land Acquisition Act (X of 1870) and
Mines (Act XVIII of 1885). With Introduction, Notes, etc. Second Edition. Enlarged and adapted for more useful reference throughout India. By H. BEVERLEY, Esq., M.A., B.C.S., one of the Judges of the High Court of Judicature, Bengal. 8vo., cloth. Rs. 6.

Landholding, and the Relation of Landlord
and Tenant, in various Countries of the World. By C. D. FIELD, M.A., LL.D., B.C.S., one of the Judges of H. M.'s High Court of Judicature in Bengal. Second Edition. 8vo., cloth. Rs. 17-12; cash 16. [1885.

N.B.—This Edition contains "The Bengal Tenancy Act," 1885, with Notes and Observations; and an Index to the whole of the Law of Landlord and Tenant in Bengal.

Introduction to the Regulations of the
Bengal Code. By C. D. FIELD. Crown 8vo. Rs. 3.
[1888.

Lectures on Indian Law upon subjects con-
nected with the Law of Landed Property in Bengal. By the Hon'ble W. MARKBY, M.A. 12mo., cloth. Rs. 3.

CONTENTS: I.—Resumption of Lands held rent-free. II.—Revenue Sale-Law of the Permanently-settled Districts. III.—Shaikast Pywust, or Alluvion and Deluvion. IV.—Charge of the person and property of minors by the Court of Wards. V.—Charge of persons and property of minors under Act XL of 1858. VI.—Of the protection which is afforded upon equitable considerations to purchasers and mortgagees when their title is impeached.

Manual of the Revenue Sale-Law, and Cer-
tificate Procedure of Lower Bengal, being Act XI of 1859; Act VII, B.C., of 1868; and Act VII, B.C., of 1880; The Public Demands Recovery Act, including Selections from the Rules and Circular Orders of the Board of Revenue. With Notes. By W. H. GRIMLEY, B.A., C.S. 8vo. Rs. 5-8; interleaved, Rs. 6.

THACKER, SPINK AND CO., CALCUTTA.

LAND AND REVENUE SALE-LAW.

Revenue Sale-Law of Lower Bengal, comprising Act XI of 1859; Bengal Act VII of 1868; Bengal Act VII of 1880 (The Public Demands Recovery Act), and the Unrepealed Regulations and the Rules of the Board of Revenue on the subject. With Notes. Edited by Wm. E. H. FORSYTH, Esq. Demy 8vo., cloth. Rs. 5.

Manual of Revenue and Collectorate Law. With Important Rulings and Annotations. By H. A. D. PHILLIPS, Bengal Civil Service. Crown 8vo., cloth. Rs. 10. [1884.

CONTENTS:—Alluvion and Diluvion, Certificate, Cesses, Road and Public Works, Collectors, Assistant Collectors, Drainage, Embankments, Evidence, Excise, Lakhiraj Grants and Service Tenures, Land Acquisition, Land Registration, Legal Practitioners, License Tax, Limitation, Opium, Partition, Public Demands Recovery, Putni Sales, Registration, Revenue Sales, Salt, Settlement, Stamps, Survey and Wards.

The Law relating to the Land Tenures of Lower Bengal. *Tagore Law Lectures*, 1875. By ARTHUR PHILLIPS, Esq. Royal 8vo., cloth. Rs. 10.

The North-Western Provinces Rent Act. With Notes, &c. By H. W. REYNOLDS, C.S. Demy 8vo. Rs. 7. [1886.

A Compendium of the Law specially relat- ing to the Taluqdars of Oudh, being the Oudh Estates Act (I of 1869); an Act to amend the Oudh Estates Act, 1869 (X of 1885); The Oudh Sub-Settlement Act (XXVI of 1866); The Oudh Taluqdars Relief Act (XXIV of 1870); and parts of the Oudh Rent Act (XIX of 1868) and the Oudh Land-Revenue Act (XVII of 1876). With a full Introduction, Notes and Appendices. By JOHN GASKELL WALKER SYKES, LL.B. (Lond.), of Lincoln's Inn, Barrister-at-Law, and Advocate, High Court, N. W. P., India, and of the Judicial Commissioner's Court, Oudh. 8vo. Rs. 8.

THACKER, SPINK AND CO., CALCUTTA.

Calcutta, March 1889.

THACKER, SPINK & CO.'S
LAW PUBLICATIONS.

Third Edition. Just Published. Royal 8vo., cloth. Rs. 16.

THE CODE OF CIVIL PROCEDURE,

ACT XIV OF 1882, AS AMENDED BY SUBSEQUENT ACTS,

WITH NOTES, APPENDICES, &c.

BY THE HON'BLE J. O'KINEALY,

One of the Judges of Her Majesty's High Court of Judicature, Bengal.

Just Published. Octavo, cloth. Rs. 16.

MEDICAL JURISPRUDENCE FOR INDIA.

BY

J. B. LYON, F.C.S., F.I.C.,

Brigade-Surgeon, Bombay Medical Service; Chemical Analyst to Government; Professor of Chemistry and Medical Jurisprudence, Grant Medical College, Bombay.

Revised as to the Legal Matter,

BY J. D. INVERARITY, ESQ.,

Barrister-at-Law.

To all those who are engaged in the administration of the law—to magistrates, lawyers, medical men, and police, as well as to students—the book will be found quite invaluable .... In the arrangement of the matter, Dr. Lyon has left nothing to be desired in the effort to render the book valuable for reference. The work is a monument of industry and research, is marked by great lucidity of exposition, and deserves, on every ground, to take rank as a standard production of its class.—*Home News.*

Third Edition. Royal 8vo., cloth. Rs. 12; Post-free, Rs. 12-6.

THE INDIAN PENAL CODE,

And other Laws and Acts of Parliament relating to the Criminal Courts of India. With Notes, &c.

Third Edition.

BY THE HON'BLE J. O'KINEALY,

One of the Judges of Her Majesty's High Court of Judicature, Bengal.

Second Edition. Royal Octavo, cloth. Rs. 18.

THE CODE OF CRIMINAL PROCEDURE,

ACT X OF 1882,

TOGETHER WITH

Rulings, Circular Orders, Notifications, etc., of all the High Courts in India; and Notifications and Orders of the Government of India and the Local Governments.

EDITED WITH COPIOUS NOTES AND FULL INDEX.

BY WILLIAM FISCHER AGNEW, ESQ.,

Barrister-at-Law;

AND GILBERT S. HENDERSON, ESQ., M.A.,

Barrister-at-Law,

Author of "*A Treatise on the Law of Succession in India.*"

Second Edition.

BY GILBERT S. HENDERSON.

"To judge from the style in which their present work is edited, the number of cases cited bearing upon the various sections, the ample notes appended where any explanation is necessary, and the full and complete indexes to the cases cited, we have little hesitation in saying that, while undoubtedly it is at present the best work on the subject, it need fear no competition in the future."—*Englishman.*

Royal Octavo, cloth. Rs. 16; Post-free, Rs. 16-9.

THE LAW OF INTESTATE AND TESTAMENTARY SUCCESSION IN INDIA,

INCLUDING

The Indian Succession Act (X of 1865), with a Commentary, and the Parsi Succession Act (XXI of 1865), the Hindu Wills' Act (XXI of 1870), the Probate and Administration Act (V of 1881), the District Delegates' Act (VI of 1881), Acts XII and XIII of 1855, the Regimental Debts' Act, 1863 (26 and 27 Vict., c. 57), the Acts relating to the Administrator-General (Acts II of 1874, XIII of 1875, and IX of 1881), the Certificate Act (XXVII of 1860), and the Oudh Estates' Act (I of 1869).

WITH NOTES AND CROSS REFERENCES.

BY GILBERT S. HENDERSON, M.A.,

Barrister-at-Law, Advocate of the High Court, Calcutta.

"We strongly recommend the book to District Judges, who have had to work Act X of 1865 rather in the dark hitherto."—*Pioneer.*

"Mr. Henderson . . . has furnished the professional and business man with a work of great practical utility."—*Civil and Military Gazette.*

Royal 8vo., Cloth. Rs. 12; *Post-free, Rs.* 12-6.

THE CODE OF CRIMINAL PROCEDURE;

BEING

A C T X O F 1882,

AS AMENDED BY

ACTS III OF 1884, X OF 1886, AND V OF 1887,

With Notes of all Judgments & Orders thereon.

Eighth Edition.

BY

THE HON'BLE H. T. PRINSEP,

Judge, High Court, Calcutta.

Second Edition. Octavo, Cloth. Rs. 6; *Post-free, Rs.* 6-4.

THE LAND ACQUISITION ACTS

(ACT X OF 1870 AND (MINES) ACT XVIII OF 1885),

WITH INTRODUCTION, NOTES, ETC.;

The whole forming a complete Manual of Law and Practice on the subject of compensation for lands taken for public purposes.

This New Edition has been adapted for more useful reference throughout British India.

By H. BEVERLEY, Esq., M.A., B.C.S.

Demy 8vo., Cloth. Rs. 8.

POSSESSION IN THE CIVIL LAW,

ABRIDGED FROM THE TREATISE OF VON SAVIGNY.

To which is added the Text of the Title on Possession from the Digest, with Notes.

COMPILED BY

J. KELLEHER, ESQ.,

Bengal Civil Service.

Just Published. Demy 8vo., Cloth. Rs. 8.

PRINCIPLES OF SPECIFIC PERFORMANCE AND MISTAKE.

BY

J. KELLEHER, ESQ.,

Bengal Civil Service.

Fifth Edition. Demy 8vo. Rs. 15.

THE INDIAN CONTRACT ACT,

NO. IX OF 1872,

TOGETHER
WITH AN INTRODUCTION AND EXPLANATORY NOTES.

Table of Cases, Contents, Appendix, &c.

By H. S. CUNNINGHAM, Esq., M.A.,
One of the Judges of H. M.'s High Court of Judicature, Calcutta;

AND

H. H. SHEPHARD, Esq., M.A.,
Barrister-at-Law.

Fifth Edition.

EDITED BY H. H. SHEPHARD, ESQ.

THE INDIAN LAW EXAMINATION MANUAL.

Third Edn., considerably enlarged with new Chapters, 8vo., cloth gilt. Rs. 5.

THE
INDIAN LAW EXAMINATION MANUAL.

By FENDALL CURRIE, Esq.,
Of Lincoln's Inn, Barrister-at-Law.

CONTENTS.

Introduction—Hindoo Law—Mahomedan Law—Indian Penal Code—Code of Criminal Procedure—Code of Civil Procedure—The Specific Relief Act—Evidence Act—Limitation Act—Succession Act—Contract Act—Registration Act—Stamp and Court Fees' Acts—Mortgage—The Easement Act—The Trust Act—The Transfer of Property Act—The Negotiable Instruments' Act.

OPINIONS OF THE PRESS.

" The experience of the compiler in the learned profession with which he is connected, speaks for the usefulness and importance of the questions that have been put in with a view to prepare candidates for the examination."
—*Indian Mirror.*

"This new edition has been rendered necessary by recent alterations in the Code of Civil Procedure, Stamp, Limitation, Registration, and other Acts, as well as by the fact that the first edition was rapidly sold off. We are not surprised that there was a large demand for the work, for it is excellently arranged."—*Englishman.*

Demy Octavo. Cloth. Rs. 10; Postage 8 ans.

THE LAW OF SPECIFIC RELIEF IN INDIA;
BEING
A COMMENTARY ON ACT I OF 1877.
By CHARLES COLLETT,

OF LINCOLN'S-INN, BARRISTER-AT-LAW, LATE OF THE MADRAS CIVIL SERVICE, AND FORMERLY A JUDGE OF THE HIGH COURT AT MADRAS; AUTHOR OF "A TREATISE ON THE LAW OF INJUNCTIONS" AND "THE LAW OF TORTS."

THIS work seeks to trace to their source, and to fully expound the equitable principles embodied in the Specific Relief Act, and will thus, it is hoped, form a compendium of equity jurisprudence adapted to, and sufficient for, the requirements of the general body of legal practitioners and officials in India.

Octavo, Cloth. Rs. 7-8; Post-free, Rs. 7-12.

THE
NEGOTIABLE INSTRUMENTS' ACT,
1881;
Being an Act to define and amend the Law relating to
PROMISSORY NOTES, BILLS OF EXCHANGE, AND CHEQUES.
EDITED BY
M. D. CHALMERS, M.A.,

Of the Inner Temple, Barrister-at-Law,
Author of "*A Digest of the Law of Bills of Exchange,*" &c., and
Editor of *Wilson's* "*Judicature Acts.*"

OPINIONS OF THE PRESS.

"From a perusal of the introduction and of the notes given to each section a clear idea of the scope and meaning of the Act is obtained, and what in the bare text was very involved becomes intelligible. Mr. Chalmers' book will, therefore, be most useful to all those who either deal in negotiable instruments in the course of their business, or who have to give legal opinions on, or conduct cases arising out of, the rights and liabilities founded on such instruments."—*Pioneer.*

1888. LEGISLATIVE ACTS. 1888.
Octavo, cloth. Rs. 4.

LEGISLATIVE ACTS
OF THE
GOVERNOR-GENERAL
IN COUNCIL,
1888.
WITH TABLE OF CONTENTS AND INDEX.

Annual Volume in continuation of *Theobald's Edition.*

Fourth Edition. Thick 8vo., cloth. Rs. 18; Post-free, Rs. 18-8.

THE
LAW OF EVIDENCE IN BRITISH INDIA.

By C. D. FIELD, M.A., LL.D.,
*Bengal Civil Service,
Recently a Judge of the High Court of Judicature, Calcutta.*

This work contains the Indian Evidence Act (as amended by Act XVIII of 1872) and all provisions on the subject of Evidence which are to be found in the Acts of Parliament applicable to India, in the Acts of the Legislative Council of India, in the Acts of the Local Legislatures of Bengal, Madras and Bombay, and in the Regulations of the Bengal, Madras and Bombay Codes, and which are in force and unrepealed by the Evidence Act or any other Act. These provisions of the Statute Law, which constitute the only rules of Evidence now in force in India, are explained in detail, and the history and meaning of the principles contained in them illustrated by the decisions of the Privy Council, of the Courts in England, and of the High Courts in India.

OPINIONS OF THE PRESS.

" This is a very interesting work, and the second edition has increased in bulk threefold as compared with the first. Mr. Field has the capacity of a master, and deals with his subject as one intimately acquainted with it. The history of the Law of Evidence in India will repay study, and, at page 12, Mr. Field begins to trace this history up to the time of the passing of the Evidence Act. . . . We have carefully looked into Mr. Field's work, and our opinion is that it is worthy of the law of which it treats, but it is made additionally and exceptionally valuable by an Introduction, which is an original essay upon evidence in general and Indian evidence in particular. His authorities, of course, are almost exclusively English, but he uses his material with skill."—*Law Times, 27th September* 1873.

" The object of the Author has been to supplement the new Act with such information as may be necessary to elucidate fully the principles on which the abstract rules contained in it are based; to illustrate the meaning, object, and application of these rules by giving some account of the origin, development, and history of the principles in question; and pointing out the different stages through which they have passed, and the alterations to which they have from time to time been subjected. This purpose is most admirably carried out in the copious notes, accompanying each section of the Code. . . . . . All outstanding rules of evidence expressly saved by the second section of the Evidence Act have been included in the volume; and as these were only to be found scattered through a multitude of different Acts and Regulations of the various Indian Legislatures, the work thus done is both extensive and important. . . . . The work in fact forms a complete Treatise on Evidence in India, arranged side by side with the express law connected with each point referred to."—*Englishman.*

" All this has been done with Mr. Field's usual care; and the copious List of Cases and ample Index render the book easy of reference and comprehension."—*Indian Daily News.*

" Mr. Field observes with great truth that 'the Codes must be administered by men whose education in law is not merely limited to the letter of the Codes themselves.'—' The rule itself,' he continues, 'will be often misunderstood, where the reason of the rule is not known.' To impart such knowledge, commentaries of this description are of great practical usefulness. . . . . The book bears abundant evidence of the labour and trouble taken in making it a complete guide."—*Hindu Patriot.*

Second Edition, demy 8vo., cl. gilt. Rs. 17-12 ; cash 16 ; Postage 12 ans.

LANDHOLDING
AND THE RELATION OF
LANDLORD AND TENANT
IN VARIOUS COUNTRIES OF THE WORLD.

By C. D. FIELD, M.A., LL.D., B.C.S.,

Late a Judge of Her Majesty's High Court of Judicature in Bengal.

CONTENTS.

The Tenure of Land and Relation of Landlord and Tenant.

I.—Early Times and under the Roman Empire—The Feudal System in Europe.
II.—England.
III.—Prussia.
IV.—France.
V.—Bavaria, Wurtemburg, Saxony, Baden, Hesse, and Saxe-Coburg-Gotha.
VI.—Belgium, the Netherlands and the Hanse Towns.
VII.—Denmark, Sweden, Geneva, and Austria.
VIII.—Italy, Sicily, and Greece.
IX.—Spain and Portugal.
X.—Russia.
XI.—Asiatic Turkey, European Turkey, and Egypt.
XII.—Ireland—Eighteenth Century.
XIII.—Ireland-Nineteenth Century.
XIV.—Ireland—Proposed Remedies.
XV.—Ireland—Legislation of 1881-1882.
XVI.—The States of America.
XVII.—Australia, Tasmania, and New Zealand.

Landholding and the Relation of Landlord and Tenant in India.

XVIII.—The Condition of Things under the Native Governments.
XIX.—From the First Settlement of the English to the Grant of the Díwání.
XX.—From the Grant of the Díwání to the Permanent Settlement.
XXI.—The Permanent Settlement.
XXII.—The Immediate Effect of the Permanent Settlement.
XXIII.—The Zemindars and Raiyats from the Permanent Settlement to 1882.
XXIV.—Acquisition and First Administration of Benares, and of Ceded and Conquered Provinces.
XXV.—The Zemindars and Raiyats from 1822 to 1859.
XXVI.—Some Account of the Settlement of the North-Western Provinces.
XXVII.—Some Account of the Tenures in the Bengal Presidency.
XXVIII.—The Rent Act of 1859.
XXIX.—Government Khas Mahals.
XXX.—The Necessity for Fresh Legislation since the Act of 1859

THE BENGAL TENANCY ACT, 1885,

With Notes and Observations, and an Index.

" We may take it that, as regards Indian laws and customs, Mr. Field shows himself to be at once an able and skilled authority. In order, however, to render his work more complete, he has compiled, chiefly from Blue-books and similar public sources, a mass of information having reference to the land-laws of most European countries, of the United States of America, and our Australasian Colonies."—*The Field.*

"Mr. Justice Field has treated his subject with judicial impartiality, and his style of writing is powerful and perspicuous."—*Notes and Queries.*

'Supplies a want much felt by the leading public men in Bengal . . . will enable controversialists to appear omniscient. On the Indian law he tells us all that is known in Bengal or applicable in this Province."—*Friend of India and Statesman.*

Important Work, by H. A. D. Phillips, Esq.

In Preparation.

COMPARATIVE CRIMINAL JURISPRUDENCE;

Showing the Law, Procedure, and Case-law of other Countries, arranged under the corresponding sections of the Indian Codes.

By H. A. D. PHILLIPS, B.C.S.

Vol. I.—**Crimes and Punishments.**
" II.—**Procedure & Police.**

The Notes in this work are arranged under the text of the Indian Criminal Codes, and are taken from the Penal and Criminal Procedure Codes of France, Belgium, Germany, Italy, Hungary, Holland, Denmark, Russia, New York, and Louisiana, from English and American Case-Law, Rulings of the Court of Cassation in Paris, and other sources.

PHILLIPS' CRIMINAL MANUAL.

Second Edition, Enlarged. Thick Crown 8vo. Rs. 10.

A MANUAL

OF

INDIAN CRIMINAL LAW;

Fully annotated, and containing all applicable Rulings of all High Courts arranged under the appropriate Sections up to date, also Circular Orders and Government Notifications.

By H. A. D. PHILLIPS, C.S.

CONTENTS.

INDIAN PENAL CODE (ACT XLV OF 1860).
CODE OF CRIMINAL PROCEDURE (ACT X OF 1882).

Evidence Act (I of 1872).
Protection of Judicial Officers Act (XVIII of 1850).
State Prisoners Act (XXXIV of 1850).
Penal Servitude Act (XXIV of 1855).
State Offences Act (XI of 1857).
State Prisoners Act (III of 1858).
Police Act (V of 1861).
Whipping Act (VI of 1864).
Post Office Act (XIV of 1866).
General Clauses Act (I of 1868).
Prisoners' Testimony Act (XV of 1869).
Cattle-Trespass Act (I of 1871).

Prisoners Act (V of 1871).
Criminal Tribes Act (XXVII of 1871).
Indian Oaths Act (X of 1873).
European Vagrancy Act (IX of 1874).
Reformatories Act (V of 1876).
Arms Act (XI of 1878).
Railways Act (IV of 1879).
Legal Practitioners Act (XVIII of 1879).
Foreign Jurisdiction Act (XIII of 1879).
Telegraph Act (XIII of 1855).
Penal Clauses of Stamp and Registration Acts.

Thacker, Spink and Co., Calcutta.

In Thick Crown Octavo. Cloth. Rs. 10; Post-free, Rs. 10-6.

MANUAL

OF

REVENUE AND COLLECTORATE LAW.

BY

H. A. D. PHILLIPS, Esq., B.C.S.,

Author of "Manual of Indian Criminal Law."

CONTAINING

Alluvion and Diluvion: Reg. XI, 1825; Act IX, 1847; Act XXXI, 1858; Act IV (B.C.), 1868.
Certificate: Act XXVII, 1860.
Cesses, Road and Public Works: Act IX (B.C.), 1880, as amended by Act II (B.C.), 1881.
Collectors, Assistant Collectors, &c.; Reg. II, 1793; Reg. XII, 1806; Reg. IV, 1821; Reg. VII, 1823; Reg. V, 1827; Act XX, 1848.
Drainage: Act VI (B.C.), 1880.
Embankments: Act II (B.C.), 1882.
Evidence: Act I, 1872, as amended by Act XVIII, 1872.
Excise: Act VII (B.C.), 1878, as amended by Act IV (B.C.), 1881, and Act I (B.C.), 1883.
Lakhiraj Grants and Service Tenures: Reg. XIX, 1793; Reg. XXXVII, 1793; Reg. II, 1819; Regs. XIII and XIV, 1825.
Land Acquisition: Act X, 1870.
Land Registration: Reg. VIII, 1800, sec. 19; Act VII (B.C.), 1876, as amended by Act V (B.C.), 1878.
Legal Practitioners: Act XVIII, 1879.
License Tax: Act II (B.C.), 1880.
Limitation: Act XV, 1877.
Minors. *See* Wards.

Opium: Reg. XX, 1817, sec. 29; Act I, 1878.
Partition: Act VIII (B.C.), 1876.
Public Demands Recovery: Reg. III, 1793; Act VII (B.C.), 1868, as amended by Act II (B.C.), 1871; Act VII (B.C.), 1880; Act XIV, 1882, secs. 278—285; 286—295; 305, 320, 322, 323, 324; 328—335; 336—343; and 344—360.
Putni Sales: Reg. VIII, 1819; Reg. I, 1820; Act VIII (B.C.), 1865.
Registration: Act III, 1877.
Revenue Sales: Act XI, 1859; Act XII, 1841; Act III (B.C.), 1862.
Salt: Act VII (B.C.), 1864, as amended by Act I (B.C.), 1873; Act XII, 1882.
Settlement: Reg. VIII, 1793; Reg. VII, 1822; Reg. IX, 1825; Reg. IV, 1828; Reg. IX, 1833; Act VIII (B.C.), 1879.
Stamps: Act I, 1879.
Survey: Act V (B.C.), 1875.
Wards: Act IX (B.C.), 1879, as amended by Act III (B.C.), 1881; Act XXXV, 1858 (Lunatics); Act XL, 1858 (Minors).

WITH NUMEROUS AND IMPORTANT

RULINGS AND ANNOTATIONS,

Extracted from English, High Court, Privy Council, and Sudder Dewani Adawlut Reports.

In Crown Octavo. Cloth. Rs. 4-4; Post-free, Rs. 4-8.

OUR
ADMINISTRATION OF INDIA,

AN ACCOUNT OF THE

CONSTITUTION AND WORKING OF THE CIVIL DEPARTMENTS
OF THE INDIAN GOVERNMENT,

With special reference to the Work and Duties of a District Officer in Bengal.

BY H. A. D. PHILLIPS, C. S.,

Author of "Manual of Indian Criminal Law," "Manual of Revenue and Collectorate Law."

"A seasonable and reasonable little book. Mr. Phillips is wholly free from the spirit of bigotry and *parti-pris* so abundantly credited to Indian Officials; no one can fail to be struck by the earnest sincerity of the book. Useful as a corrective of much mischievous and ignorant pamphleteering, it will also be of great service to all who cannot command the multitudinous Government Reports, or delve for truth in the Blue-Books."—*Saturday Review, Feb. 6th,* 1886.

"Mr. Phillips has brought together a quantity of really instructive particulars relevant to his subject. The facts which he records must, in the long run, tend to refute the allegations of the sworn enemies of the Indian Service."—*Asiatic Quarterly Review, Jan.,* 1886.

"Mr. Phillips deals with his subject in detail, his survey including the character of Land Tenures, Land-Revenue Settlements, Government Estates, Duties of Collectors, Excise, Revenue and Opium, Acquisition and Registration of Land, and other questions of equal interest and importance. He has clearly shown that the loud outcries which have been sometimes made upon our Indian Government by irresponsible people, imperfectly informed, are deserving of little or no notice."—*Manchester Courier.*

"An adequate exposition of the system of administration in India, free from all official and political bias, yet interesting enough to form a volume that will both please and instruct the reader."—*Mercantile Journal.*

"His object is to instruct the public in the system on which our Empire in India is administered. A valuable and timely publication—a noteworthy and highly creditable contribution to the discussion of Indian questions."—*Home News.*

"The excellent little book which Mr. H. A. D. Phillips has just published will be more especially serviceable to the English reader whose zeal for Indian reform sometimes goes beyond his knowledge of the subject, but it contains a great deal of information which even those who have in a convenient form a fair general acquaintance with the subject, may often find it difficult to lay their hands on. And in one respect in particular Mr. Phillips does good service, by his outspoken reference to evils of which every one is sensible, but few have the courage to denounce."—*Pioneer.*

"In eleven chapters Mr. Phillips gives a complete epitome of the civil, in distinction from the criminal, duties of an Indian Collector. The information is all derived from personal experience. A polemical interest runs through the book, but this does not detract from the value of the very complete collections of facts and statistics given."—*London Quarterly Review.*

"It contains much information in a convenient form for English readers who wish to study the working of our system in the country districts of India."—*Westminster Review.*

"A very handy and useful book of information upon a very momentous subject, about which Englishmen know very little."—*Pall Mall Gazette.*

Works by F. R. STANLEY COLLIER, C.S.
Second Edition. Crown 8vo. Cloth. Rs. 5.
THE
BENGAL LOCAL SELF-GOVERNMENT ACT
(B. C. ACT III OF 1885)
AND
THE GENERAL RULES FRAMED THEREUNDER.

With Critical and Explanatory Notes, Hints regarding Procedure, and References to the Leading Cases on the Law relating to Local Authorities. To which is added an Appendix containing the principal Acts referred to, &c., &c.; and a full Index.

BY F. R. STANLEY COLLIER, B.C.S.,
Editor of the " Bengal Municipal Manual."

CONTENTS.

Bengal Local Self-Government Act, 1885.
Rules made by the Lieutenant-Governor under the Act.
Revised Dispensary Manual. Model Rules of Business.
The Bengal Ferries Act (B. C. Act I of 1885).
The Bengal Vaccination Act (V of 1880) and Rules.
The Cattle-Trespass Act, 1871 and 1883.
The Local Authorities Loan Act, 1879, and Rules.
The Bengal Tramways Act, 1883.

Second Edition. Revised and Enlarged. Crown 8vo., cloth. Rs. 5.
THE BENGAL MUNICIPAL MANUAL
CONTAINING
THE MUNICIPAL ACT (B.C. ACT III OF 1884)
AND

Other Laws relating to Municipalities in Bengal, with the Rules and Circulars issued by the Local Government, and a Commentary.

Second Edition,
Revised and Enlarged.
BY F. R. STANLEY COLLIER, B.C.S.

CONTENTS.

1. The Bengal Municipal Act, B.C. Act III of 1884.
2. Revised Rules for the Election of Municipal Commissioners.
3. Rules for the Preparation of the Annual Administration Report.
4. Account Rules issued under s. 82.
5. Model Rules for the conduct of business at Meetings.
6. Model Pension and Leave Rules.
7. The Municipal Taxation Act, No. XI of 1881.
8. The Hackney Carriage Act, B.C., No. V of 1866.
9. An Act for Registering Births and Deaths, B.C., No. IV of 1873.
10. The Slaughter-House Act, B.C., No. VII of 1865.
11. The Cattle-Trespass Act, No. 1 of 1871.
12. The Local Authorities Loan Act, No. XI of 1879.
13. Local Authorities Loan Rules.
14. Index.

An entirely Original Work. Demy 8vo. Cloth, gilt. Rs. 12;
Post-free, Rs. 12-6.

A COMMENTARY ON HINDU LAW
OF
INHERITANCE, SUCCESSION, PARTITION, ADOPTION, MARRIAGE, STRIDHAN, AND TESTAMENTARY DISPOSITION.
BY
PUNDIT JOGENDRO NATH BHATTACHARJI, M.A., D.L.
(JOGENDRA SMARTA SIROMANI.)

All the important questions of Hindu Law are discussed in this work in accordance with those rules and principles which are recognised among Hindu jurists as beyond dispute. By going through the work, the reader will become familiar with the Hindu lawyers' modes of thought and reasoning, and will be prepared to argue or discuss any point of Hindu Law.

NOTICES.

The work before us seems to have some claims to authority which is wanting in other works that treat of the same subjects. The author has the advantage of living in the midst of the community and of having studied the subject with the additional advantage of a knowledge of Sanskrit, and the whole literature on the subject. This being so, the work under notice is likely to be consulted by all who are interested in adoption, inheritance, succession, &c., and the abilities and disabilities pertaining to rights and duties in native society.—*Indian Daily News.*

I consider the work very ably done. The principle you follow is the right one and you have worked it out with much tact and wisdom.

DR. RAJENDRA LALA MITRA.

"Babu Bhattacharji is the greatest name in the recent history of the University. He has already made his mark, having written a really original work on Hindu Law, which must assert itself against the crude compilations and false views of European writers."—*Reis and Rayyat, Decr. 26th, 1885.*

"The result of his labours is an accurate, well-arranged, comprehensive and convenient manual of Hindu Law eminently fitted to be a text-book for students, and a guide to practitioners in all cases where questions of principle are involved. Upon several important topics the book is rich in original information and observations; and we may notice particularly the Rules of Interpretations, the Legal Maxims, and the Theory of Spiritual Benefits, as remarkable for originality. . . . . The most valuable feature of the book is, that it gives us an insight into the real nature of Hindu Law, the manner in which its rules are expressed, and in which its principles must be discovered, and the methods by which its problems must be solved."—*Indian Nation.*

"It is, indeed, a new departure in the art of legal commentary. . . . .

"Our author, therefore, approaches his subject as a pundit, and brings to bear on his original authorities all the acumen which the prolonged discipline of the Nuddea school imparts to those of its pupils who have the patience to undergo its severest ordeal."—*Statesman.*

"There is thus in him a combination of high Western legal education with a masterly possession of pure Eastern legal lore gathered from the very fountain of original Sanskrit books. Such a combination is a rare thing. Yet such a combination is what is essentially wanted for a proper exposition of the Hindu Law. The superiority of the work before us to mere books of translation, such as the translation by Messrs. Colebrook, Sutherland, and Wynch, or to digests prepared by Englishmen, such as those by Messrs. Mayne, McNaughten and Cowell, is owing to such a combination of qualifications in the author of the work. . . . .

"While he has been careful to put the actual state of the Hindu Law as interpreted and assumed by our Courts, he has very largely dealt with the principles which underlie the positive texts of the two authorities in these provinces—Jimutvahan and Vijnaneshwar. He has very fully explained the systems on which these two authorities respectively proceeded. He has clearly shown wherein these authorities have been rightly understood, as also wherein they have been misunderstood."—*Amrita Bazar Patrika.*

Demy 8vo. Boards. Rs. 8; Post-free, Rs. 8-4.

A COMPENDIUM OF THE LAW
SPECIALLY RELATING TO
THE TALUQDARS OF OUDH;
BEING
THE OUDH ESTATES ACT (I) OF 1879:

An Act to amend the Oudh Estates Act, 1869 (X) of 1885; The Oudh Sub-Settlement Act (XXVI) of 1866; The Oudh Taluqdars' Relief Act (XXIV) of 1870; and parts of the Oudh Rent Act (XIX) of 1868 and the Oudh Land-Revenue Act (XVII) of 1876.

With a full Introduction, Notes, and Appendices.

BY

JOHN GASKELL WALKER SYKES, LL.B. (LOND.),
Of Lincoln's Inn, Barrister-at-Law,
and Advocate, High Court, N.-W. Provinces, India.

"An admirable compendium. The arrangement is clear, simple, and consecutive, and the selections have been made with such judgment, and are so carefully explained and elucidated that nothing essential to a thorough and accurate understanding of this form of Zemindary-Tenancy in Oudh has been omitted."—*Calcutta Review.*

Royal 8vo. Cloth. Rs. 3-8; Interleaved, Rs. 4; Postage 4 ans.

AN
INCOME-TAX MANUAL;
BEING
ACT II OF 1886.
WITH NOTES.

By W. H. GRIMLEY, B.A., C.S.,
Commissioner of Income-Tax, Bengal.

CONTENTS:—The Act, with Notes embodying the Rules of the Government of India, the Government of Bengal, and the Instructions issued by the Commissioner of Income-Tax, Bengal, under the authority of the Board of Revenue.

Rulings of the Commissioner of Income-Tax, Bengal, on references from various Districts.

Rulings and Precedents under former Income-Tax Acts in India, and under the existing Income-Tax Act in England.

Rules, Forms of Notices, Return Registers, &c.

A complete Index.

TAGORE LAW LECTURES, 1885.

Royal 8vo. Cloth, gilt. Rs. 10 ; *Post-free,* Rs. 10-10.

THE LAW RELATING TO
THE JOINT HINDU FAMILY.

By KRISHNA KAMAL BHATTACHARYYA,

Late Professor of Sanskrit in the Presidency College of Calcutta.

The Constitution of the Ancient Hindu Family and on the import of the Expression "Joint Hindu Family."
The Origin and Gradual Development of the Joint Hindu Family.
Joint Hindu Family considered as a whole.
On the Managing Member of a Joint Hindu Family.
On Limitation as affecting the Rights of the Members of a Joint Family.

On Right to Maintenance.
On the disqualified Members of a Joint Family.
On the Property of Joint Hindu Family.
Alienation of Joint Family Property.
On Son's Liability for Father's Debts.
On Partition.
On Property not liable to Partition.
Presumption in relation to Joint Hindu Family.

TAGORE LAW LECTURES, 1884.

Royal 8vo., cloth, gilt. Rs. 12 ; *Post-free,* Rs. 12-10.

THE LAW RELATING TO
GIFTS, TRUSTS, AND TESTAMENTARY DISPOSITIONS AMONG THE MAHOMMEDANS
ACCORDING TO
THE HANAFI, MALIKI, SHAFIC, AND SHIAH SCHOOLS.

COMPILED FROM

Authorities in the Original Arabic, with Explanatory Notes and References to Decided Cases, and an Introduction on the Growth and Development of Mahommedan Jurisprudence.

By SYED AMEER ALI, M.A.,

Barrister-at-Law & Author of "The Personal Law of the Mahommedans."

Importance of Mahommedan Law.
The Law relating to Gifts.
Formalities relative to Gifts.
The Revocation of Gifts.
Consideration on *Ewaz*.
The Shiah Law relating to Gifts.
The Law of Gifts according to the Shafic Doctrines.
The Law of *Wakf*.
The *Munkoof Alaihim* or the Objects of *Wakf*.

The Matwalli.
The Powers of the Wakif.
Wakf in favour of non-existing Objects.
The Principles of Construction.
The Shiah Law relating to *Wakf*.
The Maliki Law relating to *Wakf*.
The Law of *Wakf* according to Shafic School.
The Law relating to Wills.

TAGORE LAW LECTURES, 1883.

Royal 8vo. Cloth, gilt. Rs. 10 ; *Post-free, Rs.* 10-5.

THE HINDU LAW OF
INHERITANCE, PARTITION, & ADOPTION,
AS CONTAINED
IN THE ORIGINAL SANSKRIT TREATISES.
By Dr. JULIUS JOLLY, Ph.D.,
Professor of Sanskrit and Comparative Philology in the University of Würzburg.

Materials for a Historical Study of Hindu Law.
The Hindu Family System according to the Smritis.
The Early Law of Partition.
The Modern Law of Partition.

The Law of Adoption historically considered.
Unobstructed Inheritance.
Obstructed Inheritance.
The History of Female Property.
Succession to Female Property.
Exclusion from Inheritance.

TAGORE LAW LECTURES, 1882.

New Edition in Preparation.

THE LAW OF
LIMITATION AND PRESCRIPTION
IN BRITISH INDIA,
INCLUDING EASEMENTS,
WITH REFERENCES TO REPORTED CASES TO JUNE 1885.
BY
UPENDRA NATH MITTER, Esq.,
Tagore Law Lecturer, 1882, Advocate of the High Court.

TAGORE LAW LECTURES, 1881.

Royal 8vo., cloth. Rs. 12 ; *Post-free, Rs.* 12-8.

THE LAW OF TRUSTS IN BRITISH INDIA.
WITH AN APPENDIX.

The Registration of Societies Act (XXI of 1860), Religious Endowments Act (XX of 1863), Official Trustees Act (XVII of 1864), Indian Trustee Act (XXVII of 1866), The Trustees' and Mortgagees' Powers Act (XXVIII of 1866), The Religious Societies Act (I of 1880), and The Indian Trust Act (II of 1882).

By WILLIAM FISCHER AGNEW, Esq.,
Of Lincoln's Inn, Bar.-at-Law, Author of 'A Treatise on the Law of Patents,' and 'A Treatise on the Statute of Frauds.'

TAGORE LAW LECTURES, 1880.

Royal 8vo. Cloth. Rs. 16; Post-free, Rs. 16-13.

THE PRINCIPLES

OF THE

HINDU LAW OF INHERITANCE,

TOGETHER WITH

I.—A Description, and an Inquiry into the Origin of the SRADDHA Ceremonies:

II.—An Account of the Historical Development of the Law of Succession, from the Vedic Period to the present time:

III.—A Digest of the Text-Law and Case-Law, bearing on the Subject of Inheritance.

By RAJKUMAR SARVADHIKARI, B.L.,

Law Lecturer and Professor of Sanskrit, Canning College, Lucknow.

I.—Introduction.
II.—Origin and Growth of Ancestor-worship.
III.—Nature of Sraddha Rites. Persons competent to perform these Rites.
IV.—Sources of Hindu Law.
V.—Principles of Succession in the middle ages.
VI.—Principles of Succession in the middle ages (contd.).
VII.—The Modern Schools of Hindu Law.
VIII.—Modern Text-writers.
IX.—Development of the Principles of Succession from the Eleventh to the Fifteenth Century.

X.—Development of the Principles of Inheritance from the Sixteenth to the Eighteenth Century.
XI.—The Succession of an Adopted Son.
XII.—Principles of Succession under the Mitakshara Law.
XIII.—Order of Succession under the Mitakshara Law.
 I. Gotrajas.
 II. Bandhus.
 III. The Principles of Survivorship.
XIV.—Principles of Succession under the Dayabhaga Law.
XV.—Principles of Succession under the Dayabhaga Law (continued).

OPINIONS OF THE PRESS.

"To the class of readers for whom it is primarily intended, the work should prove of great value, and to those also who are no longer students in the sense of learners, but who still desire to devote their leisure hours to increase and verify their knowledge, the work in question should afford considerable interest."—*Civil and Military Gazette.*

"The volume before us forms a complete guide to the complex questions of inheritance which are continually arising, and is therefore extremely useful to law students and lawyers. But apart from its legal merits there is much to interest the general reader, both in the account given of the Sraddhas, and in the historical development of the law of succession from the Vedic ages to the present time. . . . . Before taking leave of the author, we would give as our opinion that, for a very long time, no such intelligent, clear, and masterly exposition of such a difficult branch of Hindu law as inheritance is, has been brought before the public. A far more thorough knowledge of what the true Hindu law on this subject is, will be obtained from reading this book than from wading through all the reports of decided cases that have ever been written."—*Pioneer.*

TAGORE LAW LECTURES, 1879.

Royal Octavo, cloth. Rs. 10; Post-free, Rs. 10-8.

THE LAW RELATING TO
THE HINDU WIDOW.
By Baboo TRAILOKYANATH MITRA, M.A., D.L.,
Law Lecturer, Presidency College.

- I.—The Sources of Hindu Law.
- II.—The Condition of Women and the Obligation of Widows.
- III.—The Widow's Rights of Succession.
- IV.—The Obligations of the Widow as Heir.
- V.—The Re-marriage of Widows.
- VI.—The Nature and Extent of the Widow's Estate.
- VII.—The Nature and Extent of the Widow's Estate (continued).
- VIII.—The Alienations by the Widow.
- IX.—The Alienations by the Widow (continued).
- X.—The Rights of the Reversioners.
- XI.—Suits by Reversioners.
- XII.—The Maintenance of the Widow.

TAGORE LAW LECTURES, 1878.

Royal Octavo, cloth. Rs. 10; Post-free, Rs. 10-8.

THE HINDU LAW OF
MARRIAGE AND STRIDHANA.
By Baboo GURUDASS BANERJEE, M.A., D.L.,
Tagore Law Professor.

- I.—Introductory Remarks.
- II.—Parties to Marriage.
- III.—Forms of Marriage and Formalities requisite for a valid Marriage.
- IV.—Legal consequences of Marriage.
- V.—Dissolution of Marriage—Widowhood.
- VI.—Certain Customary and Statutory Forms of Marriage.
- VII.—What constitutes Stridhan.
- VIII.—Rights of a Woman over her Stridhan.
- IX.—Succession to Stridhan, according to the Benares School.
- X.—Succession to Stridhan, according to the Maharashtra, Dravida, and Mithila Schools.
- XI.—Succession to Stridhan, according to the Bengal School.
- XII.—Succession to Woman's Property other than her Stridhan.

TAGORE LAW LECTURES, 1877.

Royal Octavo, cloth. Rs. 10; Post-free, Rs. 10-8.

THE LAW RELATING TO
MINORS IN BENGAL.
By E. J. TREVELYAN, Esq.,
Barrister-at-Law.

- I.—The Age of Majority.
- II.—The Right of Guardianship, Natural and Testamentary.
- III.—The Court of Wards.
- IV.—Appointment of Guardians by Civil Courts in the Mofussil.
- V.—Appointment of Guardians by the High Court.
- VI.—Summary Powers possessed by the Courts in Bengal with reference to the custody of Infants.
- VII.—Maintenance of Infants.
- VIII.—Liabilities of Infants.
- IX.—Duties and Powers of Guardians.
- X.—Powers of Guardians.
- XI.—Decrees against Infants; Ratification of Acts of Guardian; Limitation of Suits; Avoidance of Acts of Guardian; and Liability of Guardian.
- XII.—Some Incidents of the Status of Infancy.

TAGORE LAW LECTURES, 1876.

Second Edition. Royal Octavo, cloth. Rs. .

THE LAW OF MORTGAGE IN INDIA,

INCLUDING

THE TRANSFER OF PROPERTY ACT,

And Notes of Decided Cases brought up to date.

BY

BABOO RASHBEHARY GHOSE, M.A., D.L.,

Tagore Law Professor.

Revised and re-written to date.

CONTENTS.

Early Notions of Security.	Usufructuary Mortgage.
Hindu and Mahomedan Law of Mortgages.	Liability of Mortgagee in Possession.
Conventional Mortgages.	Liens, Legal and Judicial.
Simple Mortgages.	Subrogation.
Conditional Sales.	Pledge of Moveables.
Equity of Redemption.	Extinction of Securities.

The Transfer of Property Act, with Notes of Decided Cases.

"I take this opportunity to acknowledge the help obtained, in drawing Chapter IV of the Transfer of Property Act, from the work of another acute and learned Native lawyer, Rashbehary Ghose, *The Law of Mortgage in India*."

DR. WHITLEY STOKES,

(*Anglo-Indian Codes, Vol. I, Introd.*)

TAGORE LAW LECTURES, 1875.

Royal Octavo, cloth. Rs. 10 ; Postage, 8 annas.

THE LAW RELATING

TO

THE LAND TENURES OF LOWER BENGAL.

BY ARTHUR PHILLIPS, ESQ., M.A.,

Barrister-at-Law.

CONTENTS.

I.—The Hindoo Period.
II.—The Mahomedan Period.
III.—Akbar's Settlement.
IV.—The Zemindar.
V.—The Talookdar and other Officers. Assessment of Revenue and Rent, and their Amount.
VI.—The Payment of Revenue. Assignment of Revenue.
VII.—The English Revenue System up to the Permanent Settlement.
VIII.—The Decennial and Permanent Settlement.
IX.—Changes in the Position of the Zemindar, Intermediate Tenure-holder, and Ryot.
X.—Relative Rights of Zemindars and Holders of Under-Tenures.
XI.—The Putnee Talook. Remedies for Recovery of Revenue.
XII.—Remedies for the Recovery of Rent. Lakheraj and Service Tenures.

THE TAGORE LAW LECTURES, 1873 and 1874.

In 2 vols. Rl. 8vo., cloth, lettered. Rs. 16. Vols. sold separately, Rs. 9 each ; Postage 8 ans. each.

MAHOMEDAN LAW,
BEING
A DIGEST OF THE LAWS APPLICABLE PRINCIPALLY TO THE SUNNIS OF INDIA.
BY BABOO SHAMA CHURN SIRCAR,
Member of the Asiatic Society of Bengal.

CONTENTS.

1873.

I. Introductory Discourse.
II. Shares, Residuaries, &c.
III. Distant Kindred.
IV. Pregnancy, Missing Persons, &c.
V. Computation of Shares.
VI. The Increase and Return.
VII. Vested Inheritance, &c.
VIII. Exclusion from Inheritance, &c.
IX. Marriage.
X. Guardianship and Agency in Marriage.
XI. Dower.
XII. Fosterage, Parentage, &c.
XIII. Divorce.
XIV. Khulá, Iddat, Raját, and Re-marriage.
XV. Maintenance.
XVI. Minority and Guardianship.
XVII. Sale.
XVIII. Pre-emption.

1874.

I. On Gifts.
II. On Wasáyáh, or Wills.
III. On Executor, his Powers, &c.
IV. On Wakf, or Appropriation.
V. On the Wakf, or Appropriation of Masjids, &c.

SUMMARY OF CONTENTS OF THE IMAMIYAH CODE.

VI. Introductory Discourse.
VII. On Inheritance.
VIII. General and Special Rules of Succession.
IX. Succession.
X. Impediments to Succession.
XI. On Computation of Shares.
XII. On Permanent Marriage.
XIII. Dower, &c.
XIV. Temporary Marriage.
XV. On Divorce.
XVI. On Khulá, &c.
XVII. On the Revocation of Divorce, &c.
XVIII. On Sufá, or Pre-emption.
XIX. On Wakf, or Appropriation.

"A valuable contribution to the existing stock of information on the subject of the Mahomedan Law. .... The first elements of good writing are that a man should evince a warm interest in the subject he is treating of, and that he should know more about it than other people. These important conditions of success the learned lecturer has fully achieved. From a mature consideration of the subject, and from the possession of a vast fund of information, he is enabled to speak as one having authority. No writer, however obscure, that could throw light on his path, has been permitted by him to pass unnoticed. .... He has spared no trouble in sifting every available source of knowledge likely to elucidate that subject."—*Indian Observer.*

"The work is admirably 'got up.' In appearance it is all that a law-book should be, and its contents do not belie the promise of a fair outside. They consist of the pith of nineteen Lectures delivered in Calcutta last year by the learned author. .... In concluding the present notice we are bound to say that the Tagore Law Lectures of 1874 should form part of every lawyer's library in this country."—*Friend of India.*

THE TAGORE LAW LECTURES, 1872.

Second Edition. Demy 8vo., cloth, lettered. Rs. 6; Post-free, Rs. 6-4.

THE HISTORY AND CONSTITUTION OF THE COURTS
AND
LEGISLATIVE AUTHORITIES IN INDIA.

By HERBERT COWELL, Esq.

I. Early History—The Grant of the Dewani.
II. Early History—The Regulating Act.
III. Early History—The Settlement of 1781.
IV & V. The Legislative Council.
VI. Later History—The Presidency Town System.

VII. Later History—The Provincial Civil Courts.
VIII. The Provincial Criminal Courts.
IX. Privy Council.
X. The Superior Courts.
XI. The Inferior Civil Courts.
XII. The Inferior Criminal Courts and Police.

THE TAGORE LAW LECTURES, 1870 and 1871.

Rl. 8vo. Cl. Part I—1870, Rs. 12; Part II—1871, Rs. 8; Post-free, 8 ans. ea.

THE HINDU LAW:
BEING
A Treatise on the Law administered exclusively to Hindus by the British Courts in India.

By HERBERT COWELL, Esq.

1870.

I.—Introductory Lecture.
II.—The Position of the Hindus in the British Empire.
III.—The Hindu Family—The Joint Worship.
IV.—The Hindu Family—The Joint Estate.
V.—The Hindu Family—Its Management and Limits.
VI.—The Members of the Family—Maintenance and Guardianship.
VII.—The Members of the Family—Their Civil Status.
VIII.—The Hindu Widow.
IX.—The Right of Adoption.
X.—The Contract of Adoption.
XI.—The Right to Adopt.
XII.—Permission to Adopt—Plural Adoption.
XIII.—The Right to give in Adoption—The Qualifications for being adopted.
XIV.—The Qualifications for being adopted (continued).
XV.—The effects of Adoption.

1871.

I & II.—Alienation.
III & IV.—Partition.
V.—The Law of Succession.
VI.—The Law of Succession—Lineal Inheritance.
VII.—Collateral and Remote Succession.
VIII.—The Law of Succession—Women and Bandhus.
IX.—The Law of Succession—Exclusion from Inheritance.
X.—The Law of Succession—Exceptional Rules.
XI.—The Law of Wills; their Origin amongst Hindus.
XII.—The Law of Wills; Testamentary Powers.
XIII.—The Law of Wills.
XIV.—Construction of Wills.
XV.—On Contracts.

Demy 8vo., cloth. Rs. 7; Post-free, Rs. 7-4.

THE

NORTH-WESTERN PROVINCES RENT ACT;
BEING

ACT XII OF 1881, AS AMENDED BY ACT XIV OF 1886.

WITH NOTES, &c.

By H. W. REYNOLDS, C.S.

CONTENTS.

Rights and Liabilities of Landholders and Tenants.
Distress.
Process.
Jurisdiction of Courts.
Procedure in suits up to Judgment.

Procedure in Execution of Decrees in suits.
Appeal, Rehearing and Review.
Miscellaneous, Schedule Forms, &c.
Index of Cases and General Index.

Second Edition in the Press.

THE BENGAL TENANCY ACT:
BEING

ACT VIII OF 1885 AS AMENDED.

With Notes and Annotations, Judicial Rulings, and the Rules under the Act framed by the Local Government, the High Court, and the Registration Department.

By R. F. RAMPINI, M.A., C.S.,

Barrister-at-Law, District and Sessions Judge, Dacca;

AND

M. FINUCANE, M.A., C.S.,

Director, Agricultural Department, Bengal.

Third Edition. In Royal 8vo., Cloth. Rs. 10.

THE

INDIAN LIMITATION ACT,

ACT XV OF 1877

(*as amended by Act XII of 1879 and subsequent enactments*).

WITH NOTES.

BY

H. T. RIVAZ,

Of the Inner Temple, Barrister-at-Law, an Advocate of the High Court, N.-W. P., and of the Chief Court, Punjab.

Demy Octavo, Cloth. Rs. 5; Post-free, Rs. 5-3.

REVENUE SALE LAW

OF

LOWER BENGAL.

Comprising Act XI of 1859, Bengal Act VII of 1868, Bengal Act VII of 1880 (The Public Demands Recovery Act), and the Unrepealed Regulations and the Rules of the Board of Revenue on the subject.

EDITED WITH NOTES BY

WILLIAM E. H. FORSYTH, Esq.,
Of the Inner Temple, Barrister-at-Law.

OPINIONS OF THE PRESS.

"The work, without being pretentious, is calculated to prove exceedingly useful, and should find a place on the shelves of every one connected with land matters, as well as on the table of every lawyer."—*Indian Daily News.*

"A very useful volume."—*Statesman.*

"Forms a complete record of all the existing laws and regulations that are required to be mastered by all interested in the procedure of the law for the sale of landed properties for arrears of revenue."—*Indian Mirror.*

Demy Octavo, Cloth. Rs. 5; Post-free, Rs. 5-3.

THE

PROBATE AND ADMINISTRATION ACT;

BEING

ACT V OF 1881.

WITH NOTES.

EDITED BY THE LATE

W. E. H. FORSYTH, Esq.,
And prepared for Publication by

F. J. COLLINSON, Esq., *Barrister-at-Law.*

8vo. Rs. 5-8; interleaved, Rs. 6; Postage, 4 annas.

MANUAL OF
THE REVENUE SALE LAW
AND
CERTIFICATE PROCEDURE OF LOWER BENGAL;

Being Act XI of 1859; Act VII, B. C., of 1868; and Act VII, B. C. of 1880; The Public Demands Recovery Act, including Selections from the Rules and Circular Orders of the Board of Revenue.

WITH NOTES.

By W. H. GRIMLEY, B.A., C.S.

Octavo, Cloth. Rs. 10; Post-free, Rs. 10-6.

A TREATISE
ON THE
LAW OF BILLS OF LADING,

COMPRISING :—The various incidents attaching to the Bill of Lading, the Legal Effects of the Clauses and Stipulations, the Rights and Liabilities of Consignees, Indorsees, and Vendors under the Bill of Lading.

WITH AN APPENDIX CONTAINING FORMS, &c.

By EUGENE LEGGETT,
Solicitor.

OPINIONS OF THE PRESS.

"A useful contribution to the literature on Maritime Law."—*Law Journal.*

"The arrangement of the book is systematic and good, and the style clear and popular. There is also a good Index, and the Appendix of forms of Bills of Lading may be of use to merchants."—*Law Times.*

"The book is well written, in a clear and non-technical style."—*Liverpool Journal of Commerce.*

Octavo, Cloth. Rs. 12; Post-free, Rs. 12-6.

THE
LAW OF INDIAN RAILWAYS
AND
COMMON CARRIERS:

A COMMENTARY UPON THE INDIAN RAILWAY ACT OF 1879, THE CARRIERS' ACT OF 1865, AND THE ACT KNOWN AS LORD CAMPBELL'S ACT (XIII OF 1865).

Together with such Sections and Quotations from the Merchant Shipping Act, the Contract Act, the Railway Act, and Canal Traffic Act, Civil Procedure Code, Court-Fees' Act, and the Statute of Limitation, as apply to Carriers by Land and Water.

By W. G. MACPHERSON, ESQ.

REVIEW.

"The Author deals in a concise and succinct manner with a subject of which he is specially fitted to treat, and he seems to have spared no pains to make his work at once a reliable and exhaustive practical law-book . . . .

"The book cannot fail to command the attention and due appreciation of that portion of the community for whose edification it is more particularly intended."—*Statesman.*

POCKET EDITIONS.

NEW EDITION, REVISED, 1886.

THE POCKET PENAL CODE.
16mo. *Cloth. Rs.* 4; *Post-free, Rs.* 4-4.

THE POCKET
PENAL, CRIMINAL PROCEDURE
AND
POLICE CODES,
ALSO

THE WHIPPING ACT, AND THE RAILWAY SERVANTS' ACT;

BEING

Acts XLV of 1860 (with Amendments), X of 1882, V of 1861, VI of 1864, XXXI of 1867, and X of 1886.

WITH A GENERAL INDEX.

THE POCKET CIVIL CODE.
16mo. *Cloth. Rs.* 4; *Post-free, Rs.* 4-4.

THE POCKET
CODE OF CIVIL LAW,
CONTAINING

The Civil Procedure Code (Act XIV of 1882).
The Court-Fees' Act (VII of 1870).
The Evidence Act (I of 1872).
The Specific Relief Act (I of 1877).
The Limitation Act (XV of 1877).
The Stamp Act (I of 1879).

WITH A GENERAL INDEX,

And a Supplement containing the latest Amendments.

THE TEXT-BOOK FOR GOVERNMENT EXAMINATIONS.
Crown 8vo., cloth.   Rs. 3; Post-free, Rs. 3-3.

INTRODUCTION
TO THE
REGULATIONS OF THE BENGAL CODE.
BY C. D. FIELD, M.A., LL.D.

CONTENTS.

CHAPTER I.—The Acquisition of Territorial Sovereignty by the English in the Presidency of Bengal.
„ II.—The Tenure of Land in the Bengal Presidency.
„ III.—The Administration of Land-revenue.
„ IV.—The Administration of Justice.

Thick Octavo.   Rs. 11; cash 10; Postage, 8 ans.

THE PRACTICE
OF THE
PRESIDENCY COURT OF SMALL CAUSES OF CALCUTTA,
UNDER THE
PRESIDENCY SMALL CAUSE COURTS' ACT (XV OF 1882),
WITH NOTES AND AN APPENDIX.
BY R. S. T. MACEWEN, ESQ.,
Of Lincoln's Inn, Barrister-at-Law, one of the Judges of the Presidency Court of Small Causes of Calcutta.

PART I.—General Outline of Practice.
„ II.—The Presidency Small Cause Courts' Act (XV of 1882), with Notes.
„ III.—The Code of Civil Procedure (XIV of 1882), as extended to the Small Cause Court of Calcutta, with Notes.
„ IV.—The Rules of Practice of the Court.
„ V.—Appendix: Containing Rules defining the powers and duties of Ministerial Officers and for the transaction of business; the Local Limits of Calcutta; Schedules of Forms; Rules relating to References to the High Court; Table of institution and Court Fees; Table of Fees for Legal Practitioners; Scale of expenses to witnesses, and other information.

Octavo, cloth.   Rs. 5.

THE
INDIAN REGISTRATION ACT,
1877.
Annotated, and Reports of Cases decided upon the various Sections,
WITH NOTES, INDEX, &c.
BY CARR-STEPHEN, ESQ.,
Of Lincoln's Inn, Barrister-at-Law.

Reduced in Price to Rs. 7; Post-free, Rs. 7-14.

WITH

A Supplement containing the amended Sections in Act XII of 1879, and Act XIV of 1882.

THE
CODE OF CIVIL PROCEDURE
(ACT X OF 1877),
WITH NOTES AND APPENDIX.

By the Hon'ble L. P. DELVES BROUGHTON.

SUMMARY OF CONTENTS:

PREFACE. TABLE OF CASES. CODE OF CIVIL PROCEDURE.

APPENDIX.

Courts of Civil Judicature established in India; the Chartered High Courts at Calcutta, Bombay and Madras, and in the North-Western Provinces; Acts of Parliament and Letters Patent of 1865 and 1866. Courts not established by Charter, in Bengal, in Madras, in Bombay, in the Punjab, in British Burmah, in Oudh, in the Central Provinces, in Jhansi, in Scinde, in Aden, and in Coorg. Appeals to the Privy Council. Acts of Parliament relating to the Judicial Committee of the Privy Council. Orders in Council. Rules, High Court, Calcutta, Appellate Side and Original Side. Limitation Act. Specific Relief Act. Court-Fees' Act. Index. Index to Appendix.

OPINIONS OF THE PRESS.

"We have no hesitation in saying that, like the former work by the same author on Act VIII of 1859, the present commentary on the New Code will rank as the leading treatise on the complex subject of Indian Civil Procedure."—*Civil and Military Gazette.*

"This new edition may truly be called a great work, not only from its size, which is large even for a law-book, but from the great care which has been displayed in its preparation. . . . . . 'Every lawyer should provide himself with a copy.'"—*Englishman.*

Royal Octavo. Re. 1; Post-free, Re. 1-2.

SUPPLEMENT TO
BROUGHTON'S CIVIL PROCEDURE CODE.
THE SECTIONS OF ACT X OF 1877,

As amended by Act XII of 1879 and Act XIV of 1882, reprinted in full together with the New Sections added to the Code. Printed on one side of the paper for easy incorporation, the proper position of each Section being indicated by a reference to the page of the book.

Octavo, sewed. Rs. 4; Post-free, Rs. 4-2.

DECLARATORY DECREES,
BEING
AN EXTENDED COMMENTARY ON SECTION XV, CODE OF CIVIL
PROCEDURE, 1877.

By L. P. DELVES BROUGHTON,
Barrister-at-Law.

Royal Octavo. Cloth, lettered. Rs. 12.

AN INTRODUCTION TO THE
DUTIES OF MAGISTRATES AND JUSTICES OF THE PEACE IN INDIA.

By SIR P. BENSON MAXWELL, KT.

SPECIALLY EDITED FOR INDIA.

By THE HON'BLE L. P. DELVES BROUGHTON,
Barrister-at-Law.

Seventh Edition. 8vo. Cloth. Rs. 8; Post-free, Rs. 8-4.

THE
INDIAN EVIDENCE ACT
(ACT I OF 1872),

As amended by Act XVIII of 1872, together with Introduction
and Explanatory Notes.

BY

THE HON'BLE H. S. CUNNINGHAM, M.A.

SEVENTH EDITION.

By J. H. SPRING BRANSON, ESQ.,
Barrister-at-Law.

Second Edition. 18mo., cloth. Rs. 2; Post-free, Rs. 2-3.

A GLOSSARY
OF
MEDICAL AND MEDICO-LEGAL TERMS,

INCLUDING

THOSE MOST FREQUENTLY MET WITH IN THE COURTS.

COMPILED BY

R. F. HUTCHINSON, M.D.,
Surgeon-Major, Bengal Army.

Reduced to Rs. 7; Postage 12 ans.

INDIAN CRIMINAL DIGEST
(REVISED EDITION).

CONTAINING ALL THE IMPORTANT CRIMINAL RULINGS OF THE VARIOUS

HIGH COURTS IN INDIA
Since 1862.

With marginal Notes, giving the corresponding Sections of the present Criminal Procedure Code (Act X of 1882) wherever the Old Codes of 1861 and 1872 are quoted. Together with many English Cases which bear on the Criminal Law as administered in India.

IN FOUR PARTS:

I.—Indian Penal Code.
II.—Evidence.
III.—Criminal Procedure.
IV.—Special and Local Acts.

By J. T. HUME,
Solicitor, High Court.

Crown 8vo. Cloth. Re. 1; Postage, 2 ans.

A CHAUKIDARI MANUAL;
BEING

ACT VI, B.C., OF 1870,
AS AMENDED BY

ACTS I, B.C., OF 1871 & 1886,

Sec. 45, Code of Criminal Procedure, and s. 21, Regulation XX of 1817;

WITH

NOTES, RULES, GOVERNMENT ORDERS, AND INSPECTION NOTES.

By G. TOYNBEE, Esq.,
Magistrate of Hooghly.

Demy 8vo. Cloth. Rs. 10; Post-free, Rs. 10-4.

THE INDIAN CONTRACT ACT
(ACT IX OF 1872),

With a Commentary — Critical, Explanatory, and Illustrative.

By C. C. MACRAE, Esq., B.A.,
Of Lincoln's Inn, Barrister-at-Law.

Demy Octavo. Cloth. Rs. 6; Post-free, Rs. 6-3.

THE HINDU WILLS ACT
(ACT XXI OF 1870),
WITH

The Sections of the Indian Succession Act (Act X of 1865) made applicable to the Wills of Hindus, Jainas, Sikhs, and Buddhists, printed *in extenso* and in consecutive order.

EDITED BY

W. C. BONNERJEE,
Of the Middle Temple, Barrister-at-Law.

Demy 8vo. Cloth, gilt lettered. Rs. 8 ; Post-free, Rs. 8-4.

THE STAMP LAW OF BRITISH INDIA
AS CONSTITUTED BY THE
INDIAN STAMP ACT (No. I OF 1879);

RULINGS AND CIRCULAR ORDERS OF ALL THE HIGH COURTS, Notifications, Resolutions, Rules, and Orders of the Government of India, and of the various Local Governments, up to date; Schedules of all the Stamp Duties chargeable on Instruments in India from the earliest times.

EDITED WITH NOTES AND COMPLETE INDEX.

BY WALTER R. DONOGH, M.A.,
Of the Inner Temple, Barrister-at-Law.

"The work is the most comprehensive of its kind that we have yet seen, and no practical lawyer can afford to be without it."—*Statesman, 17th August.*

Crown Octavo. Rs. 2-4 ; cash Rs. 2 ; Postage 4 ans.

THE
INLAND EMIGRATION ACT,
WITH
ORDERS, RULES, FORMS, ETC.
Interpaged with blank pages for notes.

CONTENTS.
THE INLAND EMIGRATION ACT.

SCHEDULE OF FORMS.

ORDERS by the Lieutenant-Governor of Bengal, dated 24th February 1882.
FORMS prescribed by the Government of Bengal.
RESOLUTION of the Government of India in the Revenue and Agricultural Department, dated 27th January 1882.
RESOLUTION of the Government of Assam (Duties of Officers under Act), dated 3rd February 1882.
RULES made by the Chief Commissioner of Assam, 1883.
    Chap.   I.—Rules, Schedules, and Forms under the Inland Emigration Act.
     ,,   II.—Deputy Commissioner of Goalpara.
     ,,   III.—Dhubri Depôts.
     ,,   IV.—Transport by River Steamer.
     ,,   V.—Officers in charge of Depôts at Ports of Debarkation.
     ,,   VI.—House-Accommodation, Food, Water-supply, Medical and Sanitary Arrangements on Estates in the Labour-Districts.
     ,,   VII.—Employers.
     ,,   VIII.—Magistrates and Inspectors of Labourers.
ORDERS by the Lieutenant-Governor, N.-W. P., dated 11th July 1882.

CHEAP EDITIONS OF ACTS.

CODE OF CRIMINAL PROCEDURE (Act X of 1882.) With Table of Contents and Index. Royal 8vo. Cloth, Rs. 4; Interleaved, Rs. 5.

CODE OF CIVIL PROCEDURE (Act XIV of 1882.) With Table of Contents and Index. Royal 8vo. Cloth, Rs. 4-8; Interleaved, Rs. 5-8.

INDIAN EVIDENCE ACT; being Act I of 1872, as amended by Act XVIII of 1872. Crown 8vo. As. 12.

INDIAN LIMITATION ACT; being Act XV of 1877, as amended by Act XII of 1879. Crown 8vo. As. 8.

INDIAN STAMP ACT (No. I of 1879). Crown 8vo. As. 8.

INDIAN REGISTRATION ACT; being No. III of 1877, as amended by Act XII of 1879. Crown 8vo. As. 8.

INDIAN INCOME-TAX (Act II of 1886). With Rules by the Government of India and the Bengal Government. Table of Contents. Royal 8vo. As. 12.

INLAND EMIGRATION ACT (No. I of 1882). With Rules, Instructions, Resolution for the working of the Act, by the Revenue and Agricultural Department, the Assam Government, and the Chief Commissioner, Assam. Printed on one side only. Crown 8vo. Cloth. Rs. 2-4. Cash Rs. 2.

BENGAL TENANCY ACT (B.C., No. VIII of 1885). With Table of Contents and Index. Royal 8vo. Re. 1.

LEGISLATIVE ACTS,

Published Annually

In Continuation of Mr. Theobald's Edition. Royal 8vo. Cloth.

Acts for	1872.	With Tables of Contents and Index, Rs.				8	0
,,	1873.	,,	,,	,,	... ,,	5	0
,,	1874.	,,	,,	,,	... ,,	5	0
,,	1875.	,,	,,	,,	... ,,	5	0
,,	1876.	,,	,,	,,	... ,,	6	0
,,	1877.	,,	,,	,,	... ,,	10	0
,,	1878.	,,	,,	,,	... ,,	5	0
,,	1879.	,,	,,	,,	... ,,	5	0
,,	1880.	,,	,,	,,	... ,,	4	0
,,	1881.	,,	,,	,,	... ,,	8	0
,,	1882.	,,	,,	,,	... ,,	15	8; cash 14
,,	1883.	,,	,,	,,	... ,,	5	0
,,	1884.	,,	,,	,,	... ,,	5	0
,,	1885.	,,	,,	,,	... ,,	5	0
,,	1886	,,	,,	,,	... ,,	5	0
,,	1887	,,	,,	,,	... ,,	5	0
,,	1888	,,	,,	,,	... ,,	4	0

GRIMLEY'S EXAMINATION GUIDES.

8vo., boards. *Rs.* 4 ; *Post-free, Rs.* 4-3.

GUIDE
TO THE
SUBORDINATE CIVIL SERVICE EXAMINATIONS,
INCLUDING

A Selection from the Questions set in previous Examinations and the Orders of Government on the subject.

By W. H. GRIMLEY, Esq.

8vo., boards. *Rs.* 5 ; *Post-free, Rs.* 5-3.

RULES
FOR THE
DEPARTMENTAL EXAMINATIONS
OF

Junior Members of the Covenanted Civil Service, the Subordinate Executive Service, the Non-Regulation Commission, Police and Opium Departments; including a Selection of Examination Papers, in which are incorporated specimens of questions in Bentham's Theory of Legislation, Fawcett's Manual of Political Economy, Marshman's History of India, for the Examination of Candidates for admission into the Staff Corps, and of Officers in the Political Department.

By W. H. GRIMLEY, Esq., C.S.,
Secretary to the Central Examination Committee.

In Demy 8vo., *cloth, Rs.* 7-8 ; *Interleaved, Rs.* 8-8.

THE SEA-CUSTOMS LAW, 1878,
WITH
NOTES AND APPENDICES.
By W. H. GRIMLEY, B.A., LL.B., C.S.

PART I.—The Customs Act, with Notes.
" II.—Rules issued under the Act by the Government of Bengal and the Board of Revenue.
A List of Ports in India.
Specimens of Bills-of-Entry, Bills-of-Lading, Shipping-Bills, Manifests, Bonds, and other Documents referred to in the Act.
Table of Port-dues.
Wharf Rules.
A Collection of Miscellaneous information, Orders, and Rulings, including a Comparative Table of the Weights, Measures, and Money of the principal countries trading with India; and a Table of the Stamp-duties chargeable on Custom-house documents.
" III.—The Tariff Act.
An Alphabetical List of Articles of Import and Export, showing whether they are dutiable or free, and the denomination under which they are to be entered in the Custom-house documents.
INDEX to Customs Act, Appendices, &c.

Second Edition. Rl. 8vo. Cloth. Rs. 5; Post-free, Rs. 5-8.

THE INDIAN CONTRACT ACT
(ACT IX OF 1872)
AND
THE SPECIFIC RELIEF ACT
(ACT I OF 1877),
WITH A FULL COMMENTARY.
By D. SUTHERLAND, Esq.,
Middle Temple.

Two Volumes Imperial 8vo., Cloth.

DIGEST OF INDIAN LAW REPORTS,
A COMPENDIUM OF THE RULINGS OF THE HIGH COURT OF CALCUTTA AND OF THE PRIVY COUNCIL, 1831 TO 1876.
By D. SUTHERLAND, Esq.,
Barrister-at-Law, Middle Temple, Editor of "The Weekly Reporter," "Full Bench Rulings," "Judgments of the Privy Council," &c.
Vol. I. 1871 to 1876, Rs. 16. Vol. II. 1876 to 1881, Rs. 6.

PRIVY COUNCIL JUDGMENTS.
From 1831 to 1880.
JUDGMENTS OF THE PRIVY COUNCIL
ON
APPEALS FROM INDIA.
By D. SUTHERLAND, Esq.,
Of the Middle Temple, Barrister-at-Law.
Vol. I. 1831 to 1867. Half-calf. Rs. 12-8.
„ II. 1868 to 1877. Half-calf. Rs. 12-8.
„ III. 1878 to 1880. Half-calf. Rs. 12-8.
Or, Rs. 27-8 for the three volumes together, half-calf.

Royal Octavo. Cloth, Rs. 16; Post-free, Rs. 16-6.

THE RULES AND ORDERS
OF THE
HIGH COURT OF JUDICATURE AT FORT WILLIAM IN BENGAL, IN ITS SEVERAL JURISDICTIONS,
INCLUDING
Such of the Rules of the late Supreme and Sudder Courts as are still in force, and Forms, with an Abstract of the Charter, 14 Geo. III, the Charter Act and Charter of the High Court, the last Vice-Admiralty Commission, &c.
WITH NOTES.
By R. BELCHAMBERS,
Registrar, etc., of the High Court in its Original Jurisdiction.

www.ingramcontent.com/pod-product-compliance
Lightning Source LLC
Chambersburg PA
CBHW020859230426
43666CB00008B/1239